Unvarnished
Arkansas

Unvarnished Arkansas

The Naked Truth about Nine Famous Arkansans

Steven Teske

BUTLER
CENTER
BOOKS

BUTLER
CENTER
BOOKS

The Butler Center for Arkansas Studies
Central Arkansas Library System
100 Rock Street
Little Rock, Arkansas 72201

First Printing, March 2012

Paperback: ISBN (13) 978-1-935106-35-7
ISBN (10) 1-935106-35-x

Project manager: Rod Lorenzen
Copyeditor: Ali Welky
Book design: H. K. Stewart
Cover design: Michael Keckhaver

Library of Congress Cataloging-in-Publication Data

Teske, Steven.
  Unvarnished Arkansas : the naked truth about nine famous Arkansans / Steven
Teske.
      p. cm.
  ISBN-13: 978-1-935106-35-7 (pbk. : alk. paper)
  ISBN-10: 1-935106-35-X (pbk. : alk. paper)
  1. Arkansas--Biography. 2. Arkansas--History. I. Title.

  F410.T47 2012
  976.7--dc23

                              2011041123

Printed in the United States of America
This book is printed on archival-quality paper that meets requirements of the
American National Standard for Information Sciences, Permanence of Paper,
Printed Library Materials, ANSI Z39.48-1984.

*For the many historians who have gone before,
learning and sharing these tales …
and for all those who will come after,
continuing to learn and to share*

Table of Contents

Foreword

- A man squanders his family fortune until he is penniless, loses every time he runs for public office, and yet is so admired by the people of Arkansas that the General Assembly names a county in his honor.

- A renowned writer makes her home in the basement of a museum until she is sued by some of the most prominent women of the state regarding the use of the rooms upstairs.

- A man brings his values from the Wild West to shape a vocational school into a respected college, beginning his reform of the school with the eraser end of a pencil.

It is a cliché to say that Arkansas would not exist without its people, and another cliché says that history is all about people. But clichés become clichés because they express the truth, though often in an oversimplified manner. To the tired old argument about whether history is made by famous people like Caesar and Napoleon or whether even the greatest figures of history are products of their time and their surroundings, by now most thinkers have answered a resounding "both!" We are all the results of the places where we live and events that affect us. We all also contribute to the shape of our surroundings, sometimes deliberately, often accidentally, but always inevitably.

Over time, our own histories will be shaped again and again, as future generations try to understand us and our actions. This process of shaping and reshaping history is inevitable as well. Pedestals are built by one generation and crushed to rubble by the next. Villains are condemned by one generation, only to be rehabilitated by the next. Each change of opinion adds a new layer of varnish to the picture, with the risk that the real image of history becomes dimmer and dimmer with every change of opinion. For that matter, most researchers question whether the first opinion was, in fact, the "real" history of a person, place, or event. The layers of research may, like the layers of onion, make up the entire history and not merely serve as additions to some true core of history.

The nine people featured in this collection of biographies are not the most famous products of Arkansas. More than half of them were not even born in Arkansas, although all of them lived in Arkansas and contributed to its history and culture. Each has achieved a certain stature in local folklore, if not in the story of the state as a whole. From the pioneer who created the story of the Arkansas Traveler to the drifter who was almost a living legend—arriving unexpectedly to testify at the trial of his alleged murderers—each of these people is, in a sense, Arkansas. Each is a small part of what makes Arkansas the place it is today.

After generations of storytelling and the creation of legends, as well as years of serious scholarship into history, how can anyone remove the varnish from these lives and learn the naked truth about these people? Was Senator Solon Borland really a hot-tempered brawler who could never resist a fight? For that matter, was he truly a heroic figure who, in his many vocations (physician, newspaperman, military officer, politician, and ambassador) helped to define the southern gentleman? Was he both? Was attorney Scipio Africanus Jones really a civil rights hero in the midst of the worst era of segregation and prejudice? Or was he truly an "Uncle Tom" who learned how to "play the white man's game" so he could enrich himself, even at the expense of his fellow African Americans? Or was he both?

Perhaps the offer of unvarnished and naked truth is too bold a promise to be made. The best any writer or researcher can offer, perhaps, is the evidence and the opinions that support all the usual interpretations. For instance, some saw Charlie McDermott as a brilliant inventor who nearly built the first airplane, but others said he was eccentric, even crazy. Some insist that Sid Wallace was a desperate outlaw who deserved to be hanged, but others view him as a noble avenger, striking down the criminals who murdered his father. (Sid himself claimed that he never killed a man except in self-defense.) J. N. Smithee's friends depicted him as "generous to a fault, as brave as a lion, possessing strong convictions, and much native ability ... a good newspaper man, who did much for Arkansas." His enemies were so angered by his strong convictions and by his writing that they insulted him publicly and even shot him, trying to kill him.

Historical figures are not merely images captured in paint and hung on a wall, or captured in one agreed upon story or legend. Nor are they paper dolls whose clothing can be changed at a writer's whim. They are complex human beings, with varied motives behind their actions. In telling the story of these multi-faceted, fascinating figures, every responsible historian owes the community of researchers a record of facts that is as unvarnished, as full of naked truth, as is possible. Removing a coat of varnish reveals flaws, nicks, discrepancies, and perhaps even more varnish. For every remembered person from the past, some advocates will demand a more flattering portrait, while some detractors will insist that the portrayal has been too kind. While this conflict offers job security to researchers, writers, and historians, it is bound to create at least a small amount of dismay in those readers who wanted a truly unbiased and fact-filled history.

Every effort has been undertaken here to make these nine accounts as readable as possible, even at the expense of formal academic procedures such as footnotes. In the afterword, a brief bibliography is provided for each chapter for the benefit of readers who wish to pursue further investigation of these figures. Each of the nine is the subject of an entry in the online Encyclopedia of Arkansas History & Culture, and all nine of those encyclopedia entries are linked to additional entries about related people, places, events, and ideas. Pursuit of those materials will allow further opportunities for deeper and broader learning.

Acknowledgments

No book is written without considerable help. That is especially true of books about people or events of the past. I am particularly grateful to Marian Watson, who generously shared with me her memories of her father, Doctor John Brown Watson, as well as the details of his life that she gathered over the years from many people who worked with him. I am also grateful to Christian Beltram, who called Charles McDermott to my attention and who introduced me to McDermott's great-great-granddaughter, Lisa Reynolds. Likewise, I am grateful to Lisa and to her sister, Holly McDermott, for sharing with me their family information. I am indebted to Marcia Camp for her kindness in sharing with me so much valuable information about Bernie Babcock, and I am looking forward to reading her biography, *The Soul of Bernie Babcock*, when it is published.

The Arkansas Studies Institute is filled with many brilliant historians, and I cannot begin to name all those who have contributed in various important ways to this book. Three Butler Center staff members who deserve special thanks are Ali Welky, whose extraordinary copy-editing would improve any document; Rod Lorenzen, the manager of Butler Center Books, who has shepherded this book through many gates; and Michael Keckhaver, who far exceeded my expectations in producing the cover art for this book.

Last but not least, I am grateful to my wife Robin and our children, all of whom have been supportive during this time of research and writing and who have patiently heard these stories more times than anyone could want or deserve.

I.

Sandy Faulkner:
A Successful Failure

Sandy Faulkner represents one of the strangest paradoxes found in human society: he was a successful failure. He was tremendously popular—so popular that a county in Arkansas was named for him—and his friends included some of the most powerful political figures in Arkansas, yet Sandy often ran for office and never won an election. He was born to a wealthy family and lived the life of a wealthy gentlemen, yet he lost everything and spent his last years "penniless" and "working harder than any slave," according to a letter he wrote to his son. Sandy Faulkner is best known for a comic routine he perfected and performed at parties, that of the "Arkansas Traveler," which has inspired books, a fiddle tune (which Sandy may have written himself), and a famous painting. His renown was so great that, at his funeral, two former governors of Arkansas as well as one future governor of Arkansas served as pallbearers. Yet the same historians who delighted in telling his story could not be sure either of his correct name or the year when Sandy Faulkner was born.

Sandy Faulkner probably was born on March 3, 1803. Contrary information comes from the handwritten records of the 1850 census, which appear to indicate that he was forty-four years old at the time.

Census takers sometimes made mistakes, and they were often guilty of poor penmanship. Faulkner's age, as recorded on the paper, might be forty-seven as easily as forty-four. When a monument was placed on Sandy's grave in 1955, eighty years after he had died, the members of the Pulaski County Historical Society chose to believe the census account as they read it, and they recorded his birthdate to be March 3, 1806. That record, literally carved in stone, has been widely accepted by writers and researchers ever since it was created.

The Faulkner family—its original spelling appears to have been Falconer—had settled in the colony of Virginia, then gradually moved west, generation after generation. Sandy's parents, Nicholas Faulkner and Sally Fletcher Faulkner, were living in Scott County, Kentucky, when Sandy was born. Nicholas kept a tavern near Georgetown, Kentucky, until he decided to move farther west into Arkansas Territory around 1829. The name they gave to their son has been interpreted various ways over the years. Usually it is spelled either Sandford or Sanford. Some prominent historians of the twentieth century, including Fay Hempstead and Dallas Herndon, actually used both spellings on different pages of the same book. Contemporary sources are of little help, as they tend to refer to Sandy as "Col. S. C. Faulkner." Sometimes he is called "Sandy C. Faulkner." He generally signed his name "S. C. Faulkner." Records of the church where Sandy was baptized and where his funeral was conducted were lost in a fire. One researcher speculated that his name at birth might have been "Sanderson C. Faulkner," but no one appears to have had a guess about what name is represented by the letter C.

The solution to the mystery may lie in a box archived in the Arkansas Studies Institute in downtown Little Rock, Arkansas. Sandy Faulkner's son, Sandy Jr., moved farther west around 1860. Correspondence between Sandy Sr. (as well as the other Faulkners of Little Rock) and Sandy Jr., who was living in California, has been preserved. With them in the same box are letters written by Sandy Jr.'s daughter, Emily Evelyn Faulkner, later Emily Engelham. These letters were somehow acquired by journalist J. N. Heiskell, who left them (and many other significant historical documents) to the University of Arkansas at Little Rock. The Heiskell collection is now part of the university's archives, housed in the Arkansas Studies Institute building.

Early in the twentieth century, Emily contacted several attorneys and government offices trying to lay claim to land back in central Arkansas that had belonged to her grandfather, then to her aunt, then to a person outside the family who had been willed the land by the aunt. Emily was rebuffed by the attorneys she contacted, who did not feel she had sufficient cause to contest her aunt's will. In the exchange of letters, though, Emily distinctly identifies her father more than once as "Sandford Clinton Faulkner, Jr." Once she even names her grandfather as "Sandford Clinton Faulkner, Sr." One would think that the young lady should have known her father's true name, but it is possible she was mistaken. The issue is clouded by the fact that the first attempt to give a full name to Sandy Faulkner comes not from his granddaughter, but from Arkansas attorney E. W. Rector, who (in a letter written August 23, 1909) refers to Sandy as "Stanford Clinton Faulkner." Only after receiving that letter from Mr. Rector did Emily begin using Clinton as the middle name of her father and grandfather. The evidence is attractive, but not conclusive.

Of course, does it even matter what Sandy Faulkner called himself, or what others called him? Until the twentieth century, spellings of names were changeable, and people often spelled each other's names, and even their own names, in a variety of ways, depending on what they heard. Official documents that call him Sanford and Sandford are, in the end, equally valid. Our attention given to the "correct" spelling of a name prior to the twentieth century may, in many cases, be wasted energy.

Sandy frequently referred to himself, and was described by others, as Col. Faulkner. He had, in fact, little military service, and almost definitely was never a colonel. Faulkner did serve as aide-de-camp to the commanding general of the Second Brigade of Arkansas Militia when it was headquartered at the mouth of the White River in 1831. Serving in such a post, he almost certainly saw no military action, and even in those years, he probably spent more time managing the family plantations than he did attending to military duties. Nicholas Faulkner had purchased two cotton plantations—Linwood and Brinkley—near Point Comfort in the southeastern corner of Arkansas. The family is said to have, at one time, owned the largest number of slaves west of the Mississippi River, and no reason exists to doubt this claim.

Historian Margaret Smith Ross says that Sandy Faulkner enjoyed the life of a gentleman more than he enjoyed the management of the plantations. His chief occupations, she suggests, were hunting and fishing and other leisure activities. She describes him wandering aimlessly in the woods for days, and then returning to town to frequent taverns and engage in billiards games. Ross says that Sandy was a lover of fine horses and characterizes him as a "wild, jolly, reckless spendthrift," as well as a "splendid fiddler, always in demand." Even after his marriage around 1830 to Evelene M. Peak—the daughter of the owner of a plantation adjacent to the Faulkner land in Chicot County in southeastern Arkansas Territory—Sandy remained active in such a gentlemanly lifestyle. He was not always absent from home and hearth, though. Sandy and Evelene would raise nine children together, although only two sons and two daughters outlived their parents. Two daughters and a son died as children, and another son and daughter died as young adults.

Being a landowner with a brief military career and acting as a gentleman among gentlemen seem to have given Sandy the desire to be useful to his fellow citizens in public service. In 1833, he ran a campaign to represent Chicot County in the territorial assembly. He was defeated. After Arkansas became a state, he ran for office again, losing his campaign for the state Senate in 1854 and losing again his campaign for the state House in 1858. Family letters in 1860 reveal that he sought the office of secretary of state for Arkansas that year, but the voters chose John Stirman. Sandy was not entirely without a place in the state government, however. In 1838, the Arkansas General Assembly did appoint him commissioner of Chicot County.

A far more significant job came to Sandy at about the same time. When Arkansas became a state in 1836, its constitution created a State Bank of Arkansas and also a Real Estate Bank of Arkansas. Together, these two banks were meant to help establish stable finances for the new state. The Real Estate Bank mortgaged farm property (especially in the Delta region of eastern Arkansas, rich farmland largely devoted to raising cotton on large plantations). It also sold stock certificates and bonds and, by the end of 1839, was making loans to stockholders and also to the general public. Sandy Faulkner was president of the bank branch in Columbia in Chicot County. The branch's stockholders included wealthy and important landowners of Chicot County, including Ambrose Sevier, Anthony Davies, and Horace Walworth.

Almost from the beginning, the two banks and their administrators faced charges of fraud and corruption. Incompetence may have been a more accurate accusation. The face value of the bonds issued by the banks far exceeded the banks' assets. These bonds were sold in New York City and even made their way to Europe, where buyers expected real value as promised by the certificates. To make matters worse, the United States and Europe were in the midst of a recession in the late 1830s and early 1840s. The crisis was deepened rather than alleviated when some of the bank directors sought and received a loan of $121,000 from the North American Bank and Trust Company of New York, which happened also to be one of the major owners of the certificates. The General Assembly of Arkansas tried to bring matters back under control by naming fifteen trustees to oversee and take responsibility for the struggling bank. The trustees failed in their duties so badly that, four years later, the General Assembly passed a law that actually prohibited the incorporation or establishment of banks in Arkansas. This law remained in force until the state government was restructured at the end of the Civil War.

Sandy Faulkner would not be the last public figure in Arkansas's history to be ensnared in financial mismanagement that was not his fault. He had been chosen as bank president for the Columbia branch most likely not because he was financially astute, but merely because he was wealthy and popular. Sandy was one of the fifteen trustees chosen to salvage the bank in 1842, one of three personally responsible for the Columbia branch. That branch alone had lost nearly one million dollars of investor money. One million dollars is a large figure even today, but it was a staggeringly huge debt for the 1840s. Sandy nobly sought to extricate the bank from its debts by placing his own property in Chicot County at stake. The gamble failed. Sandy lost his plantations in southeastern Arkansas to creditors who seized the assets of the bank during its failure. Sandy surrendered all his Chicot County land, thirty-two slaves, cattle, farming implements, and sixty bales of cotton in 1851; eventually, the creditors sold all this property to recoup a portion of the debt. All the Faulkner family had left was a house and some property in the state capital of Little Rock, along with a few slaves to bring with them to that property.

Even in the midst of these dark years, though, Sandy was able to continue his life as a gentleman—and one brief event shone through these troubled years, bringing the adventure that would make Sandy Faulkner famous.

During the campaign leading up to the election of 1840, Sandy was traveling through Pope County, Arkansas, with several politicians, including Ambrose Sevier, Archibald Yell, Chester Ashley, and William S. Fulton. They came to the hut of a settler in that remote part of the state—one researcher claims to have discovered that the name of this settler was Waller Wright. Whether the travelers asked the settler for food and drink, for a place to stay the night, for directions to their destination, or merely for his vote, no one today can say for sure. Clearly, Mr. Wright (if that was indeed his name) was unwilling to give the travelers what they requested. Later, when the group had returned to Little Rock, Sandy gleefully began regaling people with the story of their encounter with the surly settler. His embellished tale of the conversation allowed the other politicians to drop out of the picture, leaving just Sandy himself, as the traveler, talking with the all-but-unresponsive squatter. Whenever Sandy told the story, he would be sure to mention that the squatter was repeatedly playing the first half of a tune on his fiddle. When Sandy, the traveler, asked why the man played only the first half of the tune without finishing it, the man responded that he did not know the second half. When Sandy then took the fiddle and completed the tune (in his version of the visit), the man was so delighted that he offered his hospitality—whiskey, food, and lodging for the night.

Whenever Sandy Faulkner told this story at parties, he inevitably finished by pulling out his fiddle and playing both parts of the tune that changed the attitude of his backwoods host. Some people say that Sandy wrote the tune himself; others think that it is an older folk tune. Whatever its source, the "Arkansas Traveler" has been named the official historical song of Arkansas. Its accompanying story is also remembered and honored, although not in an official capacity. Sandy, of course, told the story many times before anyone attempted to write it on paper; consequently, no single official version exists of the Arkansas Traveler story. Various versions have been published in a great many places. For some reason, the story was particularly popular in Ohio, and several early versions of the story and tune were published there. Often, newer versions of the story make the traveler a person from outside of Arkansas, ignoring or forgetting the fact that, in 1840, Sandy Faulkner was very much a citizen of Arkansas.

The story of the Arkansas Traveler contains much humor, with exchanges like this:

> Traveler: "Can you tell me where this road goes?"
> Squatter: "It doesn't go anywhere; every morning when I wake up, it's right outside my door."

The squatter tells the traveler that he cannot stay the night because the roof leaks and the house contains only one dry spot.

> The traveler asks, "Why don't you fix the roof?"
> The squatter says, "It's too dangerous to try to patch the roof in the rain."
> "Then why not fix the roof when it's not raining?" the traveler asks.
> In reply, the squatter says, "The roof doesn't leak when it's not raining."

In most written versions of the story, the woodsman's lines are written in hillbilly dialect and filled with poor grammar. This presentation obscures the fact that, in his original version of the story, Sandy made himself the "straight man," giving all the funny lines to his partner in the conversation. Like Bud Abbott did for Lou Costello or George Burns did for Gracie Allen, he allowed his partner to garner all the big laughs. Although in later versions of the conversation, the squatter says foolish things, Sandy's own version gave the squatter lines containing backhanded wisdom, giving him the upper hand over the traveler. Most comedians prefer to get the laughs themselves rather than setting up their partners for the best lines in the routine, but aside from his eventual triumph with the fiddle, Sandy Faulkner humbled himself in the story so he could entertain his audiences with the wit of a backwoods philosopher.

The story and the fiddle tune of the Arkansas Traveler might have been enough to guarantee fame to Sandy Faulkner, but his star rose even higher when painter Edward Washbourne decided to create

Sandy Faulkner created the story of the Arkansas Traveler, based on a conversation he had with a rural voter while Sandy was traveling around the state with a group of politicians. Most versions of his story feature a lone traveler encountering a backwoods squatter and his family at their rustic cabin. This Currier & Ives lithograph, printed around 1870, is based on an earlier painting by Edward Payson Washbourne, meant to depict the famous Arkansas Traveler legend. Courtesy of the Butler Center for Arkansas Studies, Central Arkansas Library System.

an image of Sandy's legendary conversation. Washbourne's painting shows Sandy Faulkner seated on a horse (his companions completely missing from the picture) while his partner in conversation sits in front of a dilapidated shack, surrounded by several poorly dressed children, with his wife visible through the door of the shack. A widely distributed Currier & Ives lithograph based on Washbourne's painting exaggerated even more the difference in class between the traveler and his host.

In the twentieth century, some Arkansans sought to distance the state from the legend of the Arkansas Traveler, fearing that it reinforced a negative image of Arkansas that would discourage visitors and investors. The name never fell out of favor, though, as it continued to appear as the name of newspaper columns and of magazines and even of a minor league baseball team. The Arkansas Travelers are thought to be the earliest professional sports team named for the state where they play rather than for their home city.

Sandy and his family remained in Little Rock through the 1840s and 1850s. In spite of his failures at the polls, Sandy seems to have been liked and respected in the state capital. Somehow he acquired enough land near Little Rock that he was again producing cotton through the labor of his few slaves. Sandy was invited to social events in Little Rock, not merely because of his charming story, but clearly because he was widely viewed as one of the leading citizens of the city and of the state.

The end of the 1850s saw the United States embroiled in arguments about slavery that were destined to erupt into civil war. Sandy Faulkner, a landowner who also owned slaves, was a strong advocate of "states' rights"—that is, the right of southern states to continue to make laws preserving the institution of slavery. He was not, however, so much in favor of the right of northern states to make laws *opposing* slavery, particularly when those laws meant that a slave-owner traveling in a northern state could not trust that state's government to protect his investment. In other words, if a slave escaped from his or her owner while they both were in a northern state, law enforcement officials were not required to hunt down the slave and return him or her to the owner. Northern states were even allowing former slaves to vote. Arkansas, on the other hand, passed a law by the end of the 1850s stating that a freed African American could not remain in Arkansas; any free blacks who chose to stay in the state could be seized by the government and sold back into slavery. Sandy Faulkner approved of such laws, and he approved of secession and even war to preserve such laws.

Abraham Lincoln was nominated by the Republican Party for president of the United States in 1860. Although Lincoln said that he preferred to compromise with southern slave states to preserve the

Union rather than allow them to secede, he was known as an opponent of slavery and did not receive votes from Arkansas in the election. Still, in November 1860, Lincoln won the national election. Politicians and newspapers in Arkansas urged caution, telling citizens to wait and see what would happen rather than join the rush to secede from the Union and create a Confederacy of southern, slave-owning states. The first meeting of Arkansas's secession convention decided after much debate to delay a decision and to put the matter up for vote in the summer of 1861. In spite of all this caution, though, the Civil War nearly began in Arkansas rather than in South Carolina.

In 1836, the same year that Arkansas became a state, the United States built an arsenal south of downtown Little Rock. The main building of that arsenal, which was completed in 1840, still stands today. It is a museum that commemorates, among other matters, the fact that future general Douglas MacArthur was born there in 1880. In January 1861, after Lincoln had been elected president but before his inauguration, rumors flew throughout Arkansas that the U.S. government was sending reinforcements to the arsenal, intending to hold it as federal property in the event that Arkansas seceded. Governor Harris Flanagin knew that the rumors were not true, but he could not prevent hundreds of Arkansas men from gathering in Little Rock, prepared to take the arsenal—by force if necessary—away from the U.S. government.

Captain James Totten was the commanding officer in the arsenal; he had a force of about 150 men. Like the governor, Totten knew that no reinforcements were being sent his direction. Faced with the choice of his men barricading themselves in the arsenal and resisting a potential assault or surrendering the installation, Totten decided to leave the arsenal in the hands of the State of Arkansas—after all, Arkansas was still part of the United States at that time. The grateful women of Little Rock—including Sandy's wife Evelene and their daughter Mattie—presented Captain Totten with a ceremonial sword in honor of his decision to avoid conflict in Little Rock. As a result, Fort Sumter in South Carolina has the dubious honor of being the place where the first shots of the Civil War were fired; that happened in April 1861, more than two months after a similar confrontation was avoided in Little Rock.

In 1836—the same year that Arkansas became a state—the U.S. Army acquired land for an arsenal on the south side of Little Rock. This tower is all that remains of the original arsenal. In the winter of 1861, several weeks before Arkansas seceded from the Union, secession-minded citizens gathered at the arsenal and demanded its surrender. Captain James Totten negotiated with Governor Henry Rector and peacefully handed the structure over to the state. Sandy Faulkner was made military storekeeper of the facility, a position he held until Federal troops seized Little Rock in 1863. Years later, the building and grounds were given to Little Rock as a city park, after Fort Logan Roots was built by the army north of the Arkansas River. Bernie Babcock opened the Museum of Natural History and Antiquities in the building in 1942 and lived in the basement of the structure while redecorating its rooms and setting up exhibits. The building now houses the MacArthur Museum of Arkansas Military History. Photo by Bernie Babcock, courtesy of the UALR Photograph Collection/UALR Center for Arkansas History and Culture.

After the arsenal's surrender to the State of Arkansas, Col. Sandy Faulkner was appointed its military storekeeper. He held that post during the months that Arkansas delayed its decision to secede from the Union. When war began in South Carolina, and when President Lincoln called upon Arkansas to give its share of troops to end the rebellion, the mood of Arkansas changed. Governor Flanagin sent a stiffly worded letter to the president, informing him that Arkansans would not take up arms against their fellow southerners. The convention reconvened and voted quickly (and almost unanimously) to join the Confederacy. Colonel Faulkner remained military storekeeper at the arsenal, now a Confederate post.

Sandy Faulkner remained in that position for roughly two years. His son William joined the Capital Guards, an elite Confederate unit formed in Little Rock; the next year, he died in battle. As Federal troops approached Little Rock in the summer of 1863, Sandy joined many of his fellow Arkansans in fleeing the city. The state's Confederate government relocated to Washington (the city in southern Arkansas, not the U.S. capital between Maryland and Virginia), making the Hempstead County Courthouse the new seat of state government. Sandy went farther south, relocating to Tyler, Texas, for the duration of the war.

In 1865, when the war ended and the last Arkansas Confederate troops surrendered, Sandy Faulkner returned to Little Rock. He found that he no longer had slaves to work on his cotton farm in Pulaski County, and he had no money to hire workers. Although he was able to hold on to 320 acres until 1868, eventually his farming venture failed. Like other landowners in central Arkansas, Sandy lost his land to debt and to the economic changes forced by the war. He and Evelene converted their house in the city into a boardinghouse. At this time, he wrote to Sandy Jr. in California that the two of them were "working harder than any slave" to operate the boardinghouse. Perhaps they broke even; probably they lost money. For the rest of his years, Sandy remained "penniless" according to his own account, or at least far from wealthy. When Evelene died in June 1871, Sandy continued to manage the boardinghouse with the help of a son and two daughters (both of whom had married—one more than once— but had remained in the area).

Sandy remained through this period a staunch member of the Democratic Party. He opposed the Republican administration of Arkansas and resented the political rights that were being given to freed slaves. In 1873, Sandy tried to create a new association, which he named "Old Settlers of Arkansas." He proposed that membership in the association would be restricted to people who had been citizens of Arkansas when it became a state in 1836. (This requirement would of course have eliminated any former slaves from consideration, since they had not been defined as citizens when Arkansas became a state. It also would have barred from membership anyone who had come to Arkansas from the north during or after the war.) Sandy made himself chairman of the Pulaski County branch of the association, but his effort fizzled.

Even during these hard times, though, Sandy Faulkner was not forgotten. The General Assembly was creating several new counties in Arkansas. Some were given the names of nationally prominent Republicans, including Lincoln and Grant; others received the names of prominent state Republicans during this time of Reconstruction, including Clayton and Dorsey. (Despite later efforts, Lincoln and Grant counties would retain their names; on the other hand, Clayton County would, after Reconstruction ended, be shortened to Clay County, and Dorsey County would be renamed Cleveland County.) At this time, the building of the railroad had opened up a largely uninhabited section of northern Pulaski County and eastern Conway County, and it had established a growing settlement at Conway Station. The General Assembly chose to create a new county centered at that railroad station, and they honored Sandy Faulkner by calling the new county Faulkner County.

This honor came to Sandy in 1873. The next year, Arkansas was torn apart by strife between two Republicans, Elisha Baxter and Joseph Brooks, both of whom claimed to have won the last gubernatorial election. Not being a Republican, Sandy was able to remain uninvolved in the Brooks-Baxter War, a genuine war in which more than two hundred Arkansans lost their lives before President Grant intervened. That summer, a constitutional convention met in Little Rock. The incipient state had, of course, drawn up a constitution in 1836 in order to be accepted into the United States. That constitution had been revised in 1861 when Arkansas seceded from the Union. When Little Rock was captured by Federal forces in 1863, a third constitution had been created (ratified in 1864), and that had been superseded by yet another constitution in 1868, one that bore the mark of the northerners, principally Republicans, then in charge of the state government. Now the convention was given the task of creating a constitution that would guide the state after Reconstruction and that would last for more than a few years. The convention succeeded; the current constitution of Arkansas consists of what they created in 1874, with a collection of amendments added over the years, but with the basic framework still in place.

The members of the convention knew Sandy Faulkner. They were aware that he was failing in health, and they also knew about his financial struggles. One of their first acts when they gathered in Little Rock was to give him an honorary job, complete with salary. The convention voted to name Sandy Faulkner its doorkeeper, a position he accepted with gratitude.

Around seventy years old and frail, Sandy was not able to enjoy his honor for long. On August 4, 1874, Colonel Faulkner died at his home at the corner of Commerce and Fifth streets in Little Rock. According to the *Arkansas Gazette*, the cause of his death was "gastric fever." His funeral was held at the Christian Church in Little Rock, where Sandy had recently been baptized by Rev. T. B. Lee. The convention adjourned its business so its members could attend the funeral. Eight pallbearers took part in the procession, including former Arkansas governors Henry Rector and Harris Flanagin, as well as former Confederate general Thomas Churchill, who would also one day serve as governor of Arkansas. Sandy Faulkner, like many other famous Arkansans, was buried at Mount Holly Cemetery in Little Rock. A large marker was placed at his grave in 1954, given by the Pulaski County Historical Society.

Sandy Faulkner left his mark on Arkansas history in several ways. He gave the state the story (and perhaps the tune) of the Arkansas Traveler, and his name was given to a county that would become one of the most populous counties in the state. Sandy was in many ways a symbol of Arkansas itself before and after the war. The plantations that he lost, the bank that failed under his leadership, and even his failed political campaigns all depict an Old South that never could have survived. Most importantly, though, Sandy Faulkner was never defeated by his failures. He retained a joy in living well depicted in his cheerful tale and tune of the Arkansas Traveler. For a spectacular failure, Sandy Faulkner turned out to be a remarkable Arkansas success.

II

Charlie McDermott:
He Almost Invented the Airplane

In some parts of Arkansas, this story is told and believed: at one of the first demonstrations of the Wright brothers' new airplane, after their initial success at Kitty Hawk, two men in the crowd shouted out, "Why, that's Charlie McDermott's machine!" Dr. Charles McDermott of southern Arkansas was indeed an aviation pioneer. His patented "apparatus for navigating the air" almost certainly was one of the many resources used by Orville and Wilbur Wright as they developed their famed invention. According to Charlie's granddaughter, he probably would have conquered the skies years before the Wrights if only he had had access, as they did, to a gasoline-powered engine.

"Flying Machine Charlie" was regarded by his neighbors as eccentric. He invested all his fortune trying to achieve air travel, but he also invented a cotton-picking machine, an iron hoe, and an iron wedge that is still commonly used today. He was a medical doctor, a Presbyterian elder, a plantation owner, a Greek scholar, and an early investor in Arkansas railroads. He was also a fierce defender of the Confederate cause in the Civil War, so fierce that after the war he moved for a few years to Honduras, just to keep his family from being

considered citizens of the United States after its government had
defeated the southern forces and prevented secession.

Charlie's father, Patrick McDermott, came from Ireland and
ended up in Louisiana in 1794. Patrick had left Ireland at the age of
twelve, arriving first in Baltimore, Maryland, where he was trained
as a mechanical engineer. The Spanish government then hired him
to build flour mills in Louisiana. Spain had acquired Louisiana from
France in 1763 at the end of the Seven Years' War. Now, the Spanish
gave Patrick several pieces of land, totaling roughly 2,000 acres, with
the hope that they could raise wheat in Louisiana. Patrick
established an estate on this land, which he called Waverly. He
married Emily Ozan, the Creole daughter of French settlers. Around
1800, as Napoleon Bonaparte was consolidating control of the
French government, Spain secretly returned Louisiana to France. In
1803, the U.S. government sought to buy the city of New Orleans
first from Spain and then (after learning about the secret return of
the land) from France; the United States wanted to own the city so
it could control shipping up and down the Mississippi River. Needing
money for his European adventures, Napoleon offered to sell all the
French-owned land in North America to the United States. The
American ambassador accepted the offer, and so the Louisiana
Purchase of 1803 meant that Waverly, home of the McDermott
family, was now in the United States. By this time, Patrick had
abandoned his attempts to grow wheat and instead was cultivating
sugar cane and indigo.

Charles McDermott was born to Patrick and Emily on
September 22, 1808. He had four brothers and two sisters, but all but
one brother and one sister died of illnesses while Charlie was young.
Patrick died in 1814, during the war between the United States and
Great Britain, although it does not appear that he was personally
involved in that war. The wealth of the family was invested in land
and in African slaves. The family also had $4,000 in silver coins,

which Emily hid for a time by burying them in the dirt floor of the plantation's smoke house.

As both of his parents were Roman Catholics, Charles was baptized by a Catholic priest at Point Coupee in Louisiana. His baptism in a Catholic church caused some consternation when Charles sought to join a Presbyterian congregation while he was a student at Yale University; the Presbyterians eventually recognized his Roman baptism as valid. His early Christian education came, not from his mother, but from an African slave named Tartar. This slave, who was illiterate, would ask Charles to read to him from the Bible and also had Charles help him memorize hymns. He also exhorted Charles never to be profane, nor to fish on the Sabbath, but to pray daily. Charles later wrote, "On one occasion, my mother found me on my knees, and I jumped up, much ashamed, but she commended me."

Charles maintained his religious fervor at all stages of his life. When he returned from college, he complained, "I found that I was the only young native who did not give loose to all the fashionable vices. Every form of Sabbath desecration, swearing, gambling, drinking, were the order of the day for men. Women kept their morals but knew little about the Word of God." Charles was ordained an elder in the Presbyterian Church at Woodsville, Mississippi, in 1829. He habitually studied the New Testament in its original Greek. Disappointed by the lack of spirituality in a Confederate colony he attempted to establish in Honduras following the war, Charlie wrote, "Men there do no worship … but there are two grog shops. It reminds me of Shiloh. After the Ark of God was taken by the Philistines, they fell into sin."

As a boy, Charles passed through a string of boarding schools, first in Louisiana and then in the state of New York. One of his classmates in New York was John Van Buren, son of President Martin Van Buren. Another classmate was future U.S. Supreme Court justice William Strong. (Charlie later claimed that Strong had been a thief during his student days.) Despite his many transfers from one school to another, Charles developed strong academic skills, sufficient for him to enter Yale University in 1825 and graduate with honors three years later. Returning home to Louisiana, he studied theology, law, and medicine, finally deciding to practice the last of these three disciplines. He began a medical practice as a partner of his brother-in-law, Dr. Henry Baines, who had previously practiced in a London hospital. Dr. Baines had married Charles's sister Emily while Charles was studying at Yale.

Not much has been written about Charles McDermott's medical career. He is far better remembered for his inventions and for his Arkansas plantations. It appears, though, that Charlie threw himself into medicine with the same enthusiasm that he showed for all his other avocations, determined to do well and to be up-to-date in his thinking. Unlike many frontier doctors who clung to older superstitions about health and sickness, Dr. McDermott accepted the new theory that illnesses and infections were caused by germs, living organisms too small to be seen without a microscope. He and his partner, Dr. Baines, employed new methods of sanitation in their Louisiana practice, procedures that Henry Baines had learned in London.

Meanwhile, Charles also was seeking a bride. "I felt it would be hazardous to marry for beauty or wealth," he later wrote, and so he courted first a Methodist young lady (who then chose to marry a different suitor) and then the daughter of a Presbyterian minister. When they met, she was only fourteen years old, but Charlie was sufficiently pleased with Hester Susan "Hettie" Smith that he proposed and was accepted by her and her family. They were married on December 19, 1833 (although in his later years, Charlie recorded the year as 1837); John L. Montgomery, Hettie's stepfather, conducted the ceremony.

Their oldest child, William, was born the following year (but he died young, in 1853); in the subsequent years, he was followed by fifteen brothers and sisters. Their names have been preserved in census records: Benjamin, Emily, Edward, Susan, Jane, Philip, Anabella, Charles, Catherine, Margaret, John, a second William (recorded in one census as Willie P. McDermott), a younger Edward, a younger Susan, and John Scott. It appears that some names were reused when the first bearer had died young. Charlie and Hettie also raised two nephews and two nieces after Charlie's brother Edward died; nieces Alice and Hettie are listed in the household in the 1860 census. Writers have noted that Charlie also took in orphans and raised them along with his children, so possibly Hettie was not the birth mother of all sixteen children. Abbott Kinney wrote for the *Arkansas Democrat* in 1952: "In addition to his large family, he reared a number of orphaned children, giving them the same advantages of music, dancing, and study under French masters and governesses, whom he secured on his various trips to New Orleans to buy supplies for his plantation."

In addition to practicing medicine and raising a family, Charlie also managed Waverly for his mother. For the first four years of their marriage, Charlie and Hettie made their home on fifty acres near his mother and the estate. Emily gave her son a small house, which he moved on wheels onto his fifty acres, and as the family grew, a room was added. Charlie named his tiny estate the Bee Hive, not only because of its size, but also because he actually did raise bees. He had found five hives on the family estate in 1828 and had nurtured them, increasing the number to 130 hives. Eighty of these he transported to his fifty acres, leaving the remaining fifty at Waverly. Through experience and experiment, Charlie became an expert beekeeper, selling the honey for up to twenty-five cents a pound. Meanwhile, the sugar and indigo had been displaced by cotton, the most profitable crop of the South before the end of slavery. Aside from the fifty acres, his mother gave her son no other support, except that she divided the family slaves into four equal groups, giving Charles, his brother, and their sister each one quarter of Waverly's slaves (keeping one quarter herself).

Charlie wrote in 1880 that he "became involved in debt, because of the style of expensive living in that parish of rich men" in Louisiana. As a result, he sought a more affordable place to live, with the intention of selling his portion of Waverly to pay off his debts. One day, when Charlie and his wife were visiting her family in Louisiana, Charlie was offered land on Lake Joseph, land that was rich in cotton. He noticed, though, that the overseers on the plantation were in poor health, and he also noticed high watermarks on the trees, warning him of frequent flooding in the area. Declining their offer, Charlie began to look for other land to acquire. At this point, he heard of Bayou Bartholomew in Arkansas.

The longest bayou in the world, Bayou Bartholomew meanders though southwest Arkansas for about 350 miles. Roughly 2,000 years ago, it was the main stream of the Arkansas River. But when the river changed its course, the waterway remained, with too much current to be a lake or a swamp, but too little current to be a river. The bayou was home to all sorts of freshwater creatures, and it nurtured a forest on both its banks that sheltered a great variety of wildlife as well. Now, as more settlers were entering the land, some portions were being cleared for farming, especially for cotton plantations. The bayou was the main thoroughfare for travelers and for farmers shipping their crop.

Charles was enamored with the bayou. On his first visit to Arkansas, he borrowed a horse from Sandy Faulkner and rode fifteen miles upstream to meet the settlers already living along the bayou. Gaines Landing was the principal settlement of the area, but it was little more than a river port used by the owners of the new plantations. Charlie was welcomed by the settlers, who took him hunting along the bayou. In one excursion, the group killed three bears, one wolf, one turkey, one deer, and one fox. This success at his favorite sport sold Charlie on the land. With his brother Edward as a partner, Charlie purchased land near Gaines Landing. For the next ten years, while

Edward lived in Arkansas, Charlie and his wife and children remained in Louisiana, but he frequently visited Edward for additional hunting trips and to help develop the land that would be his home.

Charlie and Edward's mother died in 1839. Her three tracts of land were divided by lot among the brothers and their sister Emily (who, like Charlie's wife, was called Hettie). Charlie had the good fortune to receive the tract that contained all the buildings of Waverly. Selling the Bee Hive, he and his wife and children moved into the family mansion, where they lived for the next five years.

By 1844, the land he had bought in Arkansas was sufficiently developed for Charlie and his wife to move north with their growing family. He then was able to sell Waverly, according to his earlier plan, and rescue himself from his accumulated debts. For seven years, the family lived in cabins near the bayou, but during those seven years, Charlie was building a fine house across the road. In 1851, they moved into that house, but a few years later, they moved again into another grand house that he had built near Monticello, Arkansas. His retreat from Bartholomew Bayou may have been prompted by fear of crime. As he later wrote, "Chicot County at that time had quite a number of 'Murrellites'—men who lived by plunder, murder, gambling, and theft. About eight of them lived near old man Fulton's house above Gaines Landing. They would steal a horse or a negro. Once they got into a quarrel with one of their own members, a man named McReynolds. Seven of them came to his place and killed him with a gun. ... Once they took a barrel of sugar from my storehouse. I prudently made no complaint." Charlie named his new estate Finisterrae, suggesting that he hoped to have finally reached the place where he would spend the rest of his life. After the Civil War broke out in 1861, though, he and his family returned to their home near the bayou.

The "Murrellites" that Charlie feared were a band of outlaws led by John A. Murrell, who was described in a local newspaper of that time as "the most daring and brazen robber who ever stripped a defenseless man or cut an innocent throat." The band was finally destroyed in 1857, after they robbed a steamboat that was carrying a large cargo of whiskey on its way down the river. The area settlers, calculating that much of the whiskey might be consumed in a short time, gathered with their muskets and engaged the inebriated thieves in a shoot-out. According to records from the time, "Not one of Murrell's men survived."

Charlie's two homes in southern Arkansas made him a natural supporter of better transportation in that part of the state. Bayou Bartholomew was fine for water travel to the Mississippi River, but the land connection between Gaines Landing and Monticello was less convenient. When a railroad was proposed that would cross the state from Gaines Landing to Texas, Charlie McDermott was among the interested investors. Later writers would call Charlie a "charter member of the Southern Pacific Railroad Company," but this description is somewhat inaccurate. The Southern Pacific (later acquired by Union Pacific) would have no presence in Arkansas until 1932, when it acquired the Cotton Belt Railroad, which in turn had earlier acquired several smaller railways, including the company in which Charlie McDermott originally invested.

Railroads were first constructed in England around the beginning of the nineteenth century; the first railroads in the United States were built in northeastern states (Maryland, Ohio, New Jersey, and New York) around 1830. The success of rail travel in those more heavily populated parts of the country caught the attention of developers in the more open western states. By 1852, several companies were being formed in Arkansas to connect its major cities to each other and to cities outside the state. Senator Solon Borland introduced legislation in Washington DC to grant land to Arkansas's incipient rail industry. Lines were planned to connect the state capital, Little Rock, to Hopefield (now West Memphis) and to Helena, both on the Mississippi River. Plans were also made for a rail line to connect Cairo, Illinois, to Fulton, Arkansas.

Plans for a southern railway developed at the same time, and the Ouachita and Red River Railroad Company was incorporated five months before the Memphis and Little Rock Railroad received its charter. Surveys were made to create a rail line from the Mississippi River to the Texas border, with stops at Fulton and at Camden. Gaines Landing was selected for the eastern terminus of the railroad, and the U.S. Senate approved Borland's land grant bill for this railroad on December 10, 1852.

Construction did not follow this legislation quickly. When the Civil War began in 1861, only a few miles of track had been laid from Gaines Landing to Collins. This short line had no locomotive train, although it did function with one hand-operated car. The line did not reach Monticello until 1879, by which time the eastern end of the line had been moved to Arkansas City, considerably north of Gaines Landing. A second line, built by the Houston, Central Arkansas & Northern Railroad, crossed the original track by the McDermott house on Bartholomew Bayou, but it was not completed until after Charlie had died. The city that sprang up at this rail crossroads retained part of his name, though, and is still called Dermott today.

The McDermott family life included music, dancing, and French masters and governesses. Life still could not have been easy for Hettie. Abbott Kinney wrote, "His wife, in addition to rearing children, had to oversee the cutting and making of clothes, and the various industries attendant to carrying on such a large estate. In her home was a nursery where the young Negro babies were kept each day under the supervision of slaves too old to work in the fields. The estate was governed with justice and kindness." Charlie built two church structures on his land near Gaines Landing: one to serve as a place of worship for his white neighbors, and the other as "a place of assemblage and instruction for his Negroes."

In spite of his Christian zeal, and in spite of his Yale education, Charlie McDermott was an ardent supporter of the institution of slavery. Although he provided a church for his slaves and child care, and easier work for the older slaves, he remained violently opposed to any suggestion that his slaves could or should live as free people. As the abolition movement grew in the northern states, Charlie became increasingly fearful of northern interference in southern plantation life. He was an aggressive advocate of secession and an outspoken supporter of the Confederacy. He did not see the Civil War as a southern rebellion; years after it ended, he still referred to it as "that terrible Yankee war." This attitude shaped all his political opinions: in 1880, he expected the second coming of Christ to occur momentarily and called upon the Kingdom of Christ to overturn "that villain Garfield" (recently elected president of the United States) and to overturn "the apostasy of the church and state," which Charlie believed had begun in 1861. Already past his fiftieth birthday when the war began, Charlie McDermott supported the war effort by continuing to operate his cotton plantation and by supporting the politicians who were leading Arkansas within the Confederate states.

Early successes gave the Federals power in the northern part of the state, and the Union eventually controlled the Mississippi River after victories at Helena and at Vicksburg, Mississippi. Their presence was not felt on the McDermott plantation until late in the conflict. One day in 1865, a friend sent a message to Charlie warning him that the Yankees were coming. Although he was ill at the time, Charlie's daughters were able to get him into a wagon and hide him in the woods to save him from being hanged by Federal troops due to his outspoken anti-Union statements. The Union soldiers entered and ransacked the home and were given orders to burn it to the ground, but reportedly a Union officer recognized a picture of Charlie and Hettie's son William and remembered him as a classmate at Yale. This mention of William may be an error, since he died in 1853 at the age of twenty, but the source says that "Young McDermott was in the Confederate Army at the time." Perhaps the recognized classmate was Benjamin McDermott, who was a sergeant in the Confederate army, or perhaps the account of the picture is entirely incorrect. The McDermott house, for whatever reason, was spared destruction at this time.

When the war ended, Charlie McDermott vowed that he would not live under the Union flag. With a friend from Louisiana named Charlie Barrow, he led a movement to found colonies of secessionists in Honduras in Central America. As a younger man, Charlie had succeeded in building a wilderness house in Arkansas, but this second experiment in carving out a new life in a strange place failed. Threatened by the hostile tropical climate and by disease (including dysentery), and disappointed by the lack of Christian religion in his fellow colonists, Charlie McDermott did not remain in Honduras. He is known to have been living there as late as 1868, but he had returned to Arkansas by the time of the federal census of 1870.

The biggest change for Charlie upon his return to Arkansas was, of course, the lack of African American slaves to work for him on the plantation. Charlie's inventiveness may not have allowed him to conquer the wilderness of Honduras, but it did not fail him in Arkansas. Charlie set to work to mechanize his plantation, and in 1874, he applied for a patent on a cotton-picking machine. Other inventors created similar devices, and Charlie's innovation in this area has not left a mark on later times, although a flattering article about his invention appeared in the *Arkansas Gazette* in January 1874. A more successful innovation from Charlie's workshop was an iron wedge that he patented in 1875. The wedge is one of the most basic tools of mankind—a hard piece of material shaped as a slender triangle, used to split apart softer material such as wood. Charlie found that a solid iron wedge was inefficient when used to split wood, and he patented a way to create a hollow iron wedge, welding plates to form a closed chamber. This wedge, one-third to one-fourth the weight of a solid wedge, was both less expensive to make and easier to use. Charlie's wedge—for which he received U.S. patent number 159,949 on February 16, 1875—is still in use all over the world in the twenty-first century. At some point in that decade, Charlie also patented an iron hoe.

Charlie McDermott is most famous, though, for U.S. patent number 133,046, issued by the government on November 12, 1872. This patent, titled "Improvement in Apparatus for Navigating the Air," is often described as the first patent ever issued for an airplane. Of course dozens if not hundreds of inventors were working in the late nineteenth century to develop some sort of flying machine. Charlie McDermott was hardly unique in either his efforts or his discoveries. All the same, Charlie was not behind the world's other inventors in his innovative work. No less an authority than *Scientific American* magazine compared Charlie's published work to the Wright brothers' machine and declared that his plans led, at least in part, to the Wrights' success.

According to family traditions, Charlie's interest in air travel consumed much of his adult life. An old oak tree at Waverly was called "Flying Charlie's Oak" because Charlie had used it as a launching pad for some of his unsuccessful early experiments. Like many nineteenth-century inventors seeking to conquer the air, Charlie observed the flight of birds, noticing especially how buzzards and cranes were able to soar for long periods of time without flapping their wings. The contraptions that Charlie built were essentially gliders, imitating the airfoil shape of a bird's wing while trying to balance the much heavier weight of a human body. Among his experimental gliders were bi-plane, tri-plane, and multi-plane models. His most successful model was a monstrosity with fifteen pairs of wings.

In 1882, Charlie was quoted in the newspapers as saying, "I hope to give a flying chariot to every poor woman, far better than Queen Victoria ever rode in. … It is mortifying that a stinking buzzard and a

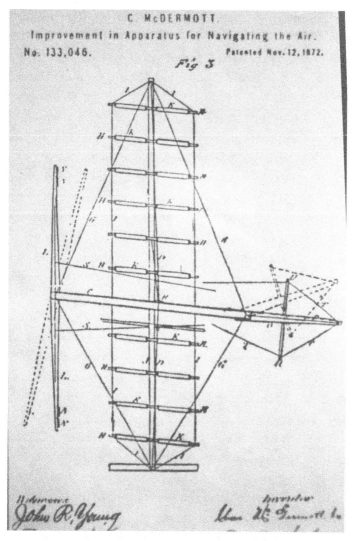

Inventor Charles McDermott filed a patent application in 1872 which included this drawing. The patent, an "Improvement in Apparatus for Navigating the Air," described a man-powered glider which he modeled in Little Rock, Chicago, and Washington DC. Many researchers believe that, had "Flying Machine Charlie" had access to gasoline-powered motors, he would have been the first to invent the airplane. The Wright brothers definitely had access to McDermott's writings, which were published in Scientific American. *Photo from the Dave Wallis Papers, courtesy of the Butler Center for Arkansas Studies, Central Arkansas Library System.*

stupid goose should fly, and man, the lord of the earth, should be any longer confided to the land and water. Many sails, one about the other, and a horizontal propulsion is the secret, which was never known until I discovered it by analysis and synthesis, and which will fill the air with flying men and women."

He made his airplanes from cypress slats that he split himself by hand and then connected with wire. The slats were made into wings with light-weight material—silk when he had more money to invest in his creations, then linen, then simple cotton cloth, and finally paper. Hettie and the older girls are said to have made themselves dresses from some of the silk scraps discarded from Charlie's earlier experiments.

The problem for Charlie was not the shape of the wings, which was easily deduced from his study of birds. The problem was to acquire sufficient speed for the wings to be effective. Most models of his design were pedal-operated like a bicycle. Often he would try to launch his machine from rooftops or other high places. Typically, he would employ boys from his family or from the neighborhood to give his machine a push while he pedaled, or even to hold the machine in place until his pedal operation had reached full speed. He also attempted to improve his odds by pointing the machine into the wind. His patent application includes this description: "The operator places himself upon the support with his face upward, his feet connected to or with the cords for actuating the propeller, and the cords of the guiding vanes in his hands, in which position he is enabled, by alternately drawing and standing outward his legs, to give a forward motion to the machine, while by means of the guiding-vane, the course of the same is also controlled." As Charlie's granddaughter, Mamie Kiblinger, later told researchers, an internal combustion engine would have made Charlie's machine practical. He had access, of course, to steam engines, but those added too much weight to the contraption. A gasoline-powered engine would have solved his problems. These were being built and improved in Europe during the same years that Charlie was working on his airplane, but the two technologies were not combined until Charlie had already died.

In the process of applying for his patent, Charlie took his thirty-wing model to Washington DC and spent nine months in the nation's capital. He also exhibited models of his aircraft at the Southeast Arkansas Fair in Monticello in 1874 and at the Arkansas State Fair in Little Rock. He brought the machine also to the Centennial Exposition at Philadelphia in 1876; reportedly, he offered a gold watch to anyone who could show him a flaw in his machine. In 1882, he announced that a practical flying machine could be built for no more than $1,000. As he was "old, feeble, and poor" (according to the newspaper ad that Charlie wrote), he begged the public for financial help to test his proposed aircraft. The money was raised and the machine was built, but the day before it was to be tested in public, a storm struck the area. The machine was lifted high into the air by the storm winds and then crashed into a tree, destroying Charlie McDermott's final hope of giving his friends and neighbors the gift of a "flying chariot."

Air travel would have to wait another generation, but already at this time, rail traffic was picking up steam. Along with the break-up of many southern plantations, the nature of southern Arkansas settlements was shaped by this innovation, which "Flying Machine Charlie" had helped to champion before the war. While he was in Honduras, a Presbyterian church was built near his Bayou Bartholomew estate and given the name New Bethany. In 1875, a post office was established at that location. At the time, it was named Bend, Arkansas, on account of the bend in the bayou, but in 1877 the name was changed to Dermott to honor Charlie. In addition to the post office and a rail station, the growing settlement included a cotton gin, a saloon, the Presbyterian church, and a mercantile store called "Morris and Kimpel." There was also a school, established after the war, for African American children. The railroad community grew rapidly and was incorporated as the city of Dermott in 1890. The city is best known for its Crawfish Festival, celebrated every year since 1984 during the third weekend of May.

Hettie McDermott died on November 13, 1880, and was buried in the McDermott family cemetery. Charlie McDermott died at his home at Dermott on October 13, 1884, suffering from a spinal disease. He was also buried in the family cemetery. During the twentieth century, the McDermott family cemetery was allowed to fall into disrepair, but in the 1960s the City of Dermott took over the land, cleaned up the cemetery, and began to maintain it as a memorial to Charles McDermott.

III

Solon Borland:
He Fought for His Honor and for His Nation

In American politics, a successful political machine requires a "loyal opposition," one or more individuals outside the machine who can be trusted to campaign against the machine, perhaps even on occasion defeat it in an election, but never damage or destroy it. This loyal opposition may be unappreciated in its own day and forgotten afterward, even if it contributes to the success of the government. The machine is remembered and is credited with all the good things (and blamed for all the bad things) that happened on its watch.

In its first twenty-five years of statehood, Arkansas had just such a political machine, the "Family" of Conways, Seviers, and Johnsons who dominated the government of Arkansas and its representation in Washington DC. The Family—related by marriage and by blood as well as by political alliance—found its loyal opposition in medical doctor and newspaperman Solon Borland. His accomplishments are often overlooked, and even his shortcomings are often forgotten, largely because he left the stage at a time when much was happening in Arkansas.

Solon Borland's greatest claim to fame rests upon his career in the U.S. Senate, taking the place of Family politician Ambrose Sevier. After his time in the Senate, Borland also achieved some notoriety as a diplomat representing the United States and President Franklin Pierce to several Central American nations, particularly Nicaragua. Borland also achieved some notice for occasional military leadership in the U.S.-Mexican War and then in the Civil War. He is remembered by some as a southern gentleman and by others as a feisty and pugnacious fighter who could never walk away from a challenge to a fistfight or a duel.

Solon Borland was born in Virginia to a physician named Thomas Wood Borland; confusion obscures his mother's precise name and Solon's birthdate. Some family records report his mother's name to be Harriet, while others say Harriett and some say Harriott. Such confusion is not unusual in early nineteenth-century American records, as we saw earlier in this book with Sandy Faulkner. Family records, church records, and government records all accepted variant spellings of names, and families would often vary the spelling of names without any effort to remain consistent. Even carved monuments such as tombstones are not reliable records of how a person spelled his or her name; such monuments would display only one of several possible spellings. And if the carver made a mistake, a family rarely would undertake the effort or pay the cost to make a correction.

Confusion about the date of Solon's birth is a little more surprising. Most of the time, when a man's birthdate is actually later than some records claim, the reason for the difference is that he lied about his age to enter the army. Solon Borland's military and political career would not have been threatened by the discovery of a deliberate error of three years; yet his official congressional biography—and his monument in Mount Holly Cemetery in Little Rock—record his birthdate to be September 21, 1808. More reliable records state that he was born on August 8, 1811. Chalk portraits drawn for the family in 1809 include Solon's two brothers but not Solon, strongly suggesting that Solon had not yet been born. It is possible that Solon lied about his age at some point to enter a school, but how this lie became part of an official record is hard to explain.

His parents clearly had high ambitions for the family. Their oldest son, Roscius Cicero Borland, was named for a classical Roman actor (often described as the "paradigm for dramatic excellence") and a classical Roman orator. Their second son, Euclid Borland, was named for the famous Greek mathematician, also a paradigm of excellence in his field. Their third son bears the name of a great Greek statesman whose name, Solon, became a synonym for sage wisdom. The family was not only ambitious but also well-informed about the classics. Thomas and his wife (until her death in 1825) most likely taught their sons at home, training them to have the same knowledge of the classics and the same respect for high achievement. Solon may have attended some college preparatory schools in North Carolina— his congressional biography says so, and a second source mentions a Hertford Academy—but his first reported formal education took place at the University of Pennsylvania Medical School in Philadelphia in 1833. He received credentials to practice medicine in 1834, and he later earned a full medical degree from a school in Louisville, Kentucky, on March 2, 1841.

Throughout his life and career, Solon Borland was known to have a firm sense of justice and a quick temper, making him liable to oppose any perceived insult against his honor. Whether this trait was true of most southern gentlemen or whether Solon helped to create this later perception of the southern gentlemen by his own excesses can be debated but not resolved. His earliest recorded fight took place in 1827 when, according to one source, he battled Murfreesboro, North Carolina, merchant James Morgan. When Morgan came at Borland with a chair, Borland reportedly stabbed Morgan with a dirk, nearly killing the merchant.

Solon Borland's first wife, like his mother, has various spellings given for her name—most often either Hildah or Huldah. They were married in Virginia in 1831. Before she died six years later, she had given birth to two sons, Harold and Thomas. In 1836 (the same year that Arkansas became a state), the four Borlands moved to western Tennessee, where Solon both practiced medicine and began a newspaper, the *Western World and Memphis Banner of the Constitution.* On July 23, 1839, Solon married Eliza Buck Hart of Memphis; they lived together as husband and wife for three years, until her death, but she bore him no children.

In 1843, the Democratic Party in Arkansas—dominated by the Family—began a newspaper in Little Rock called the *Banner.* A few weeks after the paper was founded, Solon Borland was asked to move to Little Rock and take charge of the *Banner.* He had already visited Arkansas several times since making his home in Tennessee, and it appears that he was more than willing to move both his family and his medical practice to Little Rock. The leading paper in the state at that time was the *Arkansas Gazette,* which had been founded in Arkansas Post in 1819 and moved to Little Rock when the city was designated the new territorial capital in 1821. By 1843, the paper—under the leadership of Benjamin Borden—was advocating the positions of the Whig party, which is why the Democratic Party was eager to sponsor a rival newspaper.

The differences of opinion between the two newspapers related both to local news—in which the failure of the State Bank was a key issue—and national news—mainly the presidential campaigns of Democrat James Polk and Whig Henry Clay. Both Borland and Borden wrote fiery editorials to defend their positions and to attack the opposition. When they crossed paths in the streets of Little Rock, they exchanged words in much the same spirit; Solon then lost his temper and struck Borden in the face, knocking him to the ground. The inevitable result of such an event was a challenge to a duel, which was fought on a sandbar near Fort Smith in 1844.

The custom of dueling came from Europe, where it was frequently seen as a gentlemanly way of settling a difference of opinion. Duels could be fought with any sort of weapon, including fists, swords, or guns. Essential to the spirit of dueling was the requirement that both opponents be equally armed and that the fight be witnessed by friends of both parties to ensure that neither side cheated. Most likely the custom of dueling goes back to the days of chivalry and knighthood, when it was assumed that justice would prevail in a duel, since God would not permit evil to overpower good in a fair fight. By the nineteenth century, duels were described as matters of honor. If a man (for, of course, women never fought duels) believed that his honor had been insulted, he demanded either an apology or a fight. Apologies at this stage were regarded as cowardly and embarrassing. Rather than apologize for losing his temper and striking Borden, Solon Borland was expected to meet his opponent at a predetermined place and time and, before a group of witnesses acceptable to both parties, battle until both sides were convinced that justice and honor had been preserved.

Dueling was against the law in Arkansas, so Borden and Borland had to meet outside the borders of the state. Thus they chose a sandbar near Fort Smith, the location of more than one famous duel. Borden's gun misfired and Solon remained uninjured. He, in turn, coolly aimed and fired, the bullet striking Borden in the chest, a wound that was serious but proved not to be fatal. Surgeon James Dibrell of Fort Smith dressed the wound, both sides affirmed that honor had been preserved, and they returned to Little Rock, friendly opponents rather than bitter enemies.

Solon was involved in other affairs beyond his medical work, his newspaper work, and his dueling. One of his interests, with two growing sons, was education. A member of the Masonic Lodge, Solon actively supported the creation of a Masonic school named St. Johns' College. (The odd spelling was chosen to dedicate the school to two prominent men in the New Testament, both named John. One was the cousin of Jesus, identified as John the Baptist because he baptized many people before his execution; the other was the disciple of Jesus who wrote a gospel, three epistles, and the book of Revelation.) Many institutions, including the General Assembly, misunderstood the intent of the founders and misspelled the name of the school as St. John's, leading the Masonic Lodge in Little Rock to pass a rule declaring that they would accept funding for the school even if the donors misspelled the name on their deeds of gift.

The Lodge acquired land for the school on Ninth Street in Little Rock, just east of the federal arsenal, and it received a charter from the Arkansas General Assembly on the last day of December 1850, making St. Johns' College the first chartered school in the state. Several other schools both received their charters and began classes before St. Johns' finally completed its buildings and opened to students in 1859. Closed during the Civil War and converted to a military hospital after the Federal army occupied Little Rock, the school returned to the business of education after the war until it closed for good in the 1880s. Like many institutions of the time that were called colleges, St. Johns' College was not a college in the modern sense but was more of a boarding high school for boys.

Even before St. Johns' was chartered, Solon was supporting educational endeavors in other parts of the state, especially in Dallas County, deep in the cotton fields of southern Arkansas. Solon Borland had become close friends with a French Creole schoolteacher, Madame d'Estimauville de Beau Mouchel. One source indicates that the pair were "overly friendly." She was running a finishing school for girls in Little Rock but was not doing well financially. Solon helped her to relocate to an unincorporated settlement in Dallas County, where she began a more successful girls' academy. The grateful citizens were prepared to name both the school and the community d'Estimauville in her honor, until it was revealed that she was expecting a child.

Outraged, the citizens removed her from her teaching responsibilities and required that she leave town. It was reported that "after the evidence of her 'too great intimacy' became visible, she was last seen leaving on a boat with her baby." Eventually the school and the town acquired the name Tulip, the former being fully chartered as the Tulip Female Collegiate Seminary. Meanwhile, the father of d'Estimauville's child, Solon Borland, also abandoned her, marrying instead Mary Isabel Melbourne of Little Rock on May 28, 1845. Their son George would die during the Civil War, but their daughters, Fanny and Mary, would outlive them both.

The year after Solon's third marriage began, war broke out between Mexico and the United States. The Mexican government had long been resentful of American support for the independence of Texas, and that resentment increased in 1845 when the United States added Texas as its twenty-eighth state. The presence of Zachary Taylor's troops in southern Texas drew Mexico's further ire, and fighting began in the spring of 1846. President Polk called for volunteers from Arkansas (as well as from all the other states), and Solon Borland was among those who responded. On July 4, 1846, meeting at Washington, Arkansas (in Hempstead County), a force of roughly 870 volunteers elected Congressman Archibald Yell colonel of the regiment and named Solon Borland major. The regiment traveled to San Antonio, Texas, and was sent from there into the state of Chihuahua, Mexico, crossing the Rio Grande River on October 8.

Major Borland did not achieve military glory during the war with Mexico. In fact, he and thirty-four of his men were captured on January 23, 1847, because the major had forgotten to assign nighttime guards to protect the encampment. Borland managed to escape the Mexican prisoner-of-war camp in August and did participate in the capture of Mexico City that September. As a physician, he also provided much-needed healthcare to many of the soldiers in the field. By the beginning of December, though, he had returned to Little Rock.

Here an opportunity presented itself that Major Borland was quick to seize. Senator Ambrose Sevier had served in Washington DC as one of Arkansas's two senators ever since Arkansas became a state in 1836. Now, twelve years later, Sevier was asked to assist the United States in implementing the treaty with Mexico that brought the war to an end. Borland was asked to be a "caretaker" in the Senate seat, representing Arkansas for the rest of Sevier's term until the General Assembly chose a new senator early in 1849. (U.S. senators were not elected by popular vote until the Seventeenth Amendment to the U.S. Constitution was approved in 1913. Until that year, they were chosen by state governments, since that was the original intention of the writers of the Constitution.) Borland accepted the offer of the General Assembly to complete Sevier's term. When his work in Mexico City was completed and Sevier returned to Arkansas, he hoped to be selected for a third term as senator. Borland campaigned among the legislators against Sevier, winning reelection to the position by four votes. This was one of the few times a member of the Family political machine in Arkansas was defeated by someone outside the Family. From this time on, Borland would be regarded as part of the Family's "loyal opposition" in Arkansas, first as a member of the Democratic Party, and later as an advocate for other political parties.

Solon Borland was a U.S. senator for five years. He served on the Senate's Committee on Printing and Committee on Public Lands. He also worked hard to benefit his home state. Senator Borland supported legislation to provide federal money for draining swampland in Arkansas. He supported legislation for establishing schools in Arkansas, which he promised would "yield … ample funds with which to carry out the most admirable system of common school education that can be devised." (The legislation never passed in the Senate.) He also supported legislation that divided the state into two judicial districts. The Western District judge would also oversee cases arising out of the Indian Territory that was eventually to become the state of

Oklahoma. Isaac Parker, the "Hanging Judge," was the most famous man to serve in that post, hearing cases from western Arkansas and the Indian Territory between 1875 and 1896.

Senator Borland also labored to provide a marine hospital in the state of Arkansas. The system of marine hospitals operated by the U.S. government originally was established on the eastern seaboard along the Atlantic Ocean. More recently, though, the government had decided to create similar hospitals, one near the Great Lakes and six along the major rivers of the continent. These hospitals were intended not only for military personnel but also largely for civilian workers in the boating industry. Senator Borland wanted to ensure that one of the three hospitals designated to serve workers along the Mississippi River would be located in Arkansas. He selected the city of Napoleon as a suitable site. Napoleon had been built near the point where the Arkansas River empties into the Mississippi River. It was already a notorious city by 1848 and would later be depicted in the nonfiction writing of Mark Twain, who would describe it in *Life on the Mississippi* as a "town of innumerable fights—an inquest every day; town where I used to know the prettiest girl ... and the most accomplished in the whole Mississippi Valley." Other writers also commented on its frontier-town atmosphere: rough buildings hastily built and rowdy citizens prone to various kinds of criminal activity. Napoleon was then vying with other river cities (such as St. Louis, Missouri; Memphis, Tennessee; and Vicksburg, Mississippi) to be a center for river life and commerce. Senator Borland hoped that the presence of a marine hospital would lend itself to the city's promotion.

In 1850, Congress sent army officer Stephen Harriman Long to build a marine hospital in Napoleon. Long reported back to Congress that the site was unsuitable, prone to flooding, and generally unhealthy. Prompted by Senator Borland, Congress refused to allow Long to seek a better site, even when heavy rains raised the river and flooded the construction site. Long obeyed his orders and built the hospital, but it took until 1854 to complete the building, which stood only a few years before it fell into the river. In fact, the entire city of Napoleon eventually fell into the Mississippi River. Before the river claimed the city, the Federal army had occupied Napoleon during the Civil War and had torn apart several buildings (including the county courthouse) to fuel a bonfire during a January snowstorm in 1863. A few months later, Federal forces diverted the main channel of the Mississippi River so they could avoid a Confederate ambush point on one of the many river bends in the area. The new channel aimed the force of the mighty river directly at Napoleon. The force of moving water, especially during the high-water years of 1868 and 1874, destroyed the entire city, sweeping away the marine hospital that Senator Borland had provided to his state.

Senator Borland's interests were regional as well as state-related. He was a believer in Manifest Destiny, the conviction that the United States was meant to grow in size and in power, dominating North America "from sea to shining sea." He also believed in the institution of slavery and in the right of each state government to preserve this institution if it so chose. During the debates surrounding the complicated legislation known as the Compromise of 1850, Senator Borland held a strongly pro-southern and pro-slavery position. More than a decade before the secession of South Carolina led to the beginning of the Civil War, Borland was already giving speeches in Arkansas suggesting that it was better to depart the nation than to compromise and weaken the southern states. The serious illness of his wife, following the death of their niece while she was being tended in their household, kept Borland from actually being present in the Senate while the key votes were held narrowly approving the Compromise of 1850. His political opponents later used this absence to claim that Senator Borland secretly agreed with the compromise but was afraid to make that position public.

The same sense of honor that had caused Solon Borland to exchange gunshots with newspaperman Borden also drew attention to the senator during his political career. He engaged in a fist-fight with Senator Henry Foote of Mississippi, although fist-fights were not particularly remarkable with Foote, who had once drawn a gun on the Senate floor and threatened Senator Thomas Hart Benton of Missouri. In 1852, Borland punched Joseph Kennedy, superintendent of the United States Census, because Kennedy had interrupted a conversation Borland was having with Senator James Pearce of Maryland and printer Lem Towers. Reportedly, Senator Borland was removed from the Senate Committee on Printing as a result of the unfavorable publicity following this incident.

Even when he was home in Arkansas, Senator Borland was not immune to controversy. Various newspaper reports describe an incident at the Anthony House, a prominent Little Rock hotel, during which gunshots were fired. The fight was the culmination of a long series of arguments (some spoken but many printed in the newspapers) trading accusations of political corruption and of misbehavior, in several cases going back to the Mexican War. According to some accounts, Solon's only participation in the event was an effort to break up the brawl, which involved several political leaders and newspaper figures including *Banner* editor Lambert Whitley, his junior editor Lambert Reardon, Arkansas state auditor Christopher Columbus Danley, Pulaski County sheriff Benjamin Danley, and their brother William Danley, who was a steamboat engineer. Writers for the *Banner*, however, insisted that the Danleys and Senator Borland had intended to assassinate editor Whitley. The senator was required to post bond (although he ended up being out of town during the trial), and the *Gazette* suggested that the entire fight was due to political competition between Senator Borland and Congressman Robert Ward Johnson, a Family politician.

In 1850, Senator Borland voted against the Clayton-Bulwer Treaty, an agreement between the United States and Great Britain which would, among other things, prevent either nation from acquiring land in Central America to build a canal connecting the Atlantic and Pacific oceans. The senator believed that Great Britain was already barred from such activity by the Monroe Doctrine, and his unshaken belief in Manifest Destiny led him to avow that the United States should consider itself entitled to acquire such land. However this conviction was perceived by others, it clearly was welcome to some American leaders. When Franklin Pierce won the election of 1852 and was inaugurated as the fourteenth president of the United States in 1853, he named Solon Borland the new ambassador of the United States to Nicaragua and the first U.S. ambassador to Costa Rica, Honduras, and Guatemala. Of course Borland had to resign his position in the U.S. Senate to begin his diplomatic career. He did so, and the Arkansas General Assembly chose Robert Ward Johnson to replace Solon Borland in the Senate.

Solon Borland was outspoken about his political convictions during the months he served as ambassador. Speaking from Managua, Nicaragua, he called upon the U.S. government to repudiate the Clayton-Bulwer Treaty. In a later speech in Nicaragua, he announced that his ambition was to encourage the annexation of Nicaragua by the United States, saying that the land would form "a bright star in the flag of the United States." He also declared that Honduras should receive the support of the United States in its conflict with Great Britain. In fact, Solon Borland had been sent to these southern nations at a particularly tense time in their history. Following the Revolutionary War that had made Britain's thirteen colonies an independent country, the colonies of Spain and Portugal had also sought and achieved their independence. Controlled by a few wealthy owners of land, whose property included plantations, mines, and many slaves, these new countries occasionally battled each other in border

Solon Borland came to Arkansas in 1843 to edit the Arkansas Banner, *a newspaper supporting the Democratic politicians who controlled most of the state government before the Civil War. Already an experienced newsman, Borland was also a physician with some military experience. He became an officer during the Mexican War and then was appointed to a position in the U.S. Senate. He was later the U.S. ambassador to Nicaragua, and he became an officer in the Confederate army in 1861. In every phase of his multi-faceted career, Borland found himself at odds, often violently, with his peers.* This is his official portrait as U.S. senator, courtesy of the Library of Congress, Daguerreotype Collection, Prints and Portraits Division.

disputes. For the most part, they all continued supplying European nations with raw materials such as sugar, coffee, cotton, wool, beef, hardwoods, and precious metals. Meanwhile, Great Britain was expanding its empire, making inroads into Africa and India and establishing trading rights in China. Canada, Australia, and New Zealand were also part of the British Empire, making the slogan "The sun never sets on the British Empire" quite true. The British government coveted the plantation lands in the Caribbean Sea and in Central and South America. Britain already possessed the island of Jamaica, and it had claimed a settlement on the mainland that it called British Honduras. (It is now the nation of Belize.) Britain also had established a colony on the South American coast which is now Guyana. For his part, Solon Borland felt an obligation to oppose the growth of the British Empire in the Western Hemisphere.

Secretary of State William Marcy reprimanded the ambassador for some of his controversial public statements, and Solon Borland had already resigned his post and was preparing to leave for home when he was faced with the most severe crisis of his diplomatic career. The British had, in 1848, seized a Nicaraguan city called San Juan del Norte, renaming it Greytown and placing officials from Jamaica in charge of its government. An American citizen, Cornelius Vanderbilt, had contracted with Great Britain to build a canal across Nicaragua that was to start in Greytown. Ambassador Borland had been struggling to cancel any Nicaraguan agreement with Great Britain and to ensure that any canal built in that land would remain the property of the United States. Now, as Borland was leaving, local authorities attempted to arrest a Captain Smith (a citizen of the United States and a passenger on the ambassador's ship), saying that he had shot and killed a sailor on another ship after their two ships collided. Solon refused to allow the officials of Greytown to board the ship, reportedly leveling a rifle at the officials seeking to make the arrest. (According to one source, Solon had grabbed this rifle out of the hands of one of the Jamaican officials in the arresting party.) In return, the officials refused to allow the ship to leave the harbor, and Solon himself was threatened with arrest (although he had diplomatic immunity and was never actually placed under arrest). At some point during the argument, a bottle was thrown at the ambassador, slightly wounding Solon on the head and giving him a permanent scar. Solon eventually made his escape and reported the incident in Washington DC, strongly recommending a response by the U.S. government.

Acting upon former ambassador Borland's recommendation, the United States dispatched the USS *Cyane*, a naval sloop-of-war, to Greytown. The ship arrived on July 13, 1854, and the crew found that the city had been abandoned. They proceeded to bombard and destroy the city. The U.S. government was asked by Great Britain and others to apologize for the incident but refused to do so; early in 1855, President Pierce did issue a statement saying that he would have preferred that the incident had been resolved without the use of force, but that "the arrogant contumacy of the offenders rendered it impossible to avoid the alternative either to break up their establishment or to leave them impressed with the idea that they might persevere with impunity in a career of insolence and plunder." The destruction of Greytown has been described by some historians as "an early example of gunboat diplomacy," while others have suggested that it was an action made necessary by the need to resist British expansionism.

Meanwhile, Solon Borland returned to Little Rock, opening a medical practice and operating a drugstore. By the summer of 1855, he was also writing again for the *Gazette*. Before leaving for Central America in 1853, Solon had bought an interest in that paper, which now was supporting the American Party. This new political group, which was also known as the "Know-Nothing Party," had won some local elections in other parts of the country with its platform of limiting immigration (especially from predominately Roman Catholic countries) and insisting on the use of English as the only language of the United States. In 1856 it nominated former president Millard Fillmore, who lost the election to James Buchanan of the Democratic Party. In the southern states, the American Party was presented as a better choice than either the pro-slavery Democratic Party or the anti-slavery Republican Party, but Solon probably supported the American Party largely out of opposition to the Family. The American Party did not do well in Arkansas, and Solon spent the next four years more focused on his medical practice and newspaper work than on politics.

After spending time with relatives in New Orleans, Borland returned to Memphis, although in 1858 he moved his wife and children to a house built on land that he owned in Princeton, Arkansas. They were not far from Tulip, where Solon's mistress once had lived. In Memphis, Solon reopened his medical practice and acquired yet another newspaper, the *Memphis Enquire*. He ran for a position in the Tennessee legislature, but lost that election on February 9, 1861. After that loss, Solon sold the *Enquire* and returned to Arkansas.

Even before running for public office in Tennessee, Solon had campaigned in Arkansas for the Constitutional Union Party, which nominated John Bell for president. Solon Borland must have been pleased with the aftermath of the 1860 election in Arkansas, even though Republican Abraham Lincoln won the presidency over John Bell and the other candidates. In Arkansas, Henry Rector was elected governor. He defeated Richard Johnson, the brother of Robert Ward Johnson, making Rector the first governor of the state who was openly against the Family. (Family members James Conway and Elias Conway were the first and fifth governors of Arkansas; between their terms, the three elected governors were largely compromise candidates neither for nor against the Family. Ironically, Rector technically was part of the Family, being a cousin to James and Elias Conway. Still, he declared himself openly opposed to the Family machine.)

Moreover, the question of secession was being raised in Arkansas even before shots were fired at Fort Sumter in South Carolina. In

February, the military arsenal in Little Rock was surrendered to a citizens' group representing the state of Arkansas, and in April, Solon Borland was selected by Governor Rector as his aide-de-camp to take the federal military installation at Fort Smith in northwestern Arkansas. Borland was provided with 235 soldiers in five companies to travel up-river in three steamboats to Fort Smith. More soldiers joined the force in Van Buren, leading some historians to estimate that Borland was in command of a thousand men by the time he reached Fort Smith. The state had not yet formally declared its secession, but the commander of the fort, Captain Samuel Sturgis, decided to abandon the installation before Borland and his militia arrived. Borland and his band returned to Little Rock, with great rejoicing at every stop along with way throughout their river journey. In the capital city, the group was disbanded, although many of the soldiers later assembled into the Capital Guards, which was involved in many significant Civil War actions.

Borland was not given any significant new assignments following the vote of Arkansas's convention to secede from the Union. Nevertheless, he labored to recruit soldiers to fight for Arkansas and the Confederacy. Many of his recruits were gathered into the Third Arkansas Infantry, one of the most active Confederate units from Arkansas. On July 24, Borland was named the Confederate commander for northeastern Arkansas. Colonel Borland made the city of Pocahontas his base and traveled around the region to inspect military preparedness to resist invasion from the north.

He resigned from his position the next January after a confrontation with Governor Rector. Colonel Borland had been trying to prevent prices from getting out of hand due to speculation by declaring an embargo upon goods. The governor rescinded the colonel's order. Solon replied that the governor had no authority to countermand a Confederate officer, but Rector's position was upheld by the Confederate secretary of war Judah P. Benjamin. Indicating that he was experiencing health problems, Colonel Borland then resigned his post and, by the summer of 1862, he was again a practicing doctor in Little Rock.

From this point on, Solon Borland's fortunes only went downhill. His son George—who, for a time, served under William Woodruff Jr., as did newspaperman J. N. Smithee—died of illness on June 24 while serving in Indian Territory under General Albert Pike. Solon's wife Mary died in October. Solon and his daughters relocated to the property he now rented in Princeton in Dallas County, Arkansas; they moved some time before the Federal army captured the city of Little Rock in September 1863. That month, Solon moved again, this time to Harris County, Texas. Recognizing his failing health—he was suffering from pneumonia—Solon wrote his will on the last day of 1863. He divided his property between his daughters, Fannie and Mary, noting that his only surviving son, Harold, was "already grown, of mature age, and so provided for in profession and education. ... Besides, he is a man and they are girls, and I should consider it an insult to him, to deprive them of anything for his benefit, and a wound to his strong and generous fraternal affection." The property in question included a tract of land in Drew County, Arkansas, three African American slaves, two mules, furniture, about $5,000 that he had already left with a Mrs. Holmes in Princeton for his daughters' support, and "most important of all," $25,800 in Confederate States Bonds.

The next day, January 1, 1864, Solon Borland died. He is buried in Texas, but the location of his grave is unknown. A monument to his memory was erected in Mount Holly Cemetery in Little Rock. The location of the monument is evidently the family plot where his wife Mary and their son George were both buried, as well as Solon's son Thomas from his first marriage. The monument, which was placed by the Arkansas Bar Association in 1992, incorrectly states that Solon Borland was born in 1809.

At the time of Borland's death, the state of Arkansas was sufficiently distracted by the Civil War that little was done to mark his passing beyond notices in various newspapers. The turmoil of Reconstruction also prevented politicians from the Family or opposed to the Family from commenting on the loss of Solon Borland. After the war, new political issues involving carpetbaggers from the north and divisions within the Republican Party pushed deceased politicians far out of the attention of the public. After many years of service to the state of Arkansas, Solon Borland had the misfortune to become one of its most forgotten political leaders.

IV.

J. N. Smithee:
He Didn't Just Write the News;
Some Days He Was the News

Two newspaper editors crossed paths on the streets of Little Rock Sunday morning, May 5, 1878. Shots rang out. J. N. Smithee of the *Arkansas Democrat* fell to the sidewalk, injured. John Adams, editor of the *Arkansas Gazette*, stood over Smithee, brandishing his revolver. Cursing each other, the man vented their anger. "If it weren't for your wife and children I'd finish you, you ... slanderer," Adams growled, and Smithee reportedly answered, "Finish me!"

J. N. Smithee was not "finished" in 1878. He continued in his chosen careers of newspaper work and politics until he died of a self-inflicted gunshot on Independence Day in 1902. During his sixty years, Smithee contributed to several Arkansas newspapers, held the office of land commissioner in Arkansas, ran for governor of the state, was chosen as the first president of the Arkansas Press Association, and was involved in several of the most violent confrontations in Arkansas during the nineteenth century.

James Newton Smithee was born near Smithville, Arkansas, on January 11, 1842. Smithville at that time was in Lawrence County; it

Before the merger of the Arkansas Gazette and the Arkansas Democrat in 1991, the newspapers coexisted for more than a hundred years, often fighting a bitter press war with each other. J. N. Smithee began the Democrat in the spring of 1878. A few weeks later, he was shot in a duel with John Adams, editor of the Gazette, in a Sunday morning gunfight on the streets of Little Rock. A politician who served as Arkansas's land commissioner and later ran for governor, Smithee eventually acquired control of the Gazette, editing the paper for roughly three years just before the end of the nineteenth century. This image of Smithee appears courtesy of the Butler Center for Arkansas Studies, Central Arkansas Library System.

is now in Sharp County, which was not formed until 1868. Throughout his professional career, Smithee was known by his initials, J. N. Even some of his family members believed that his nickname, Jasper, was his real name. His parents, Samuel Harris Smithee and Edna Elizabeth (Woodrow) Smithee, were farmers of Scottish-Irish background; the family had first come to North America during the colonial era, before the American Revolution. J. N. Smithee had only three months of formal education, which he received in a country schoolhouse in Lawrence County. The rest of his knowledge he picked up on his own.

Smithee had his first newspaper job at age twelve. He learned the printing trade as an apprentice at a new newspaper, the *Des Arc Citizen*. Printing and newspapers had been established in Arkansas even before Smithee was born. William Woodruff had brought the first printing press to Arkansas Post in 1819 and had started the state's first newspaper, the *Arkansas Gazette*, that year. When the territorial government chose to move its capital up the river to higher ground at the "little rock," Woodruff packed up his printing press and moved too, publishing the first Little Rock editions of the *Gazette* in December 1821. His example inspired other newspapers all over Arkansas. Des Arc, situated on a bayou extending north from the White River about fifty miles east of Little Rock, did not have a newspaper until 1854, when John Morrill began the *Citizen*; young Smithee was probably a member of the staff from the first printing of the newspaper. (One reliable source reports that, even before the *Citizen* was published, Smithee received some training in typesetting at the *Pine Bluff Republican*.)

A common cliché describes a career newspaperman as having printers' ink running in his veins. This could apply as easily to Smithee as to anyone. After completing his apprenticeship at the *Des Arc Citizen*, he worked a few months at the *Powhatan Advertiser*, then was found again in the newspaper business in Pine Bluff. By 1860, Smithee had saved enough money to purchase a half interest in a paper. He acquired the *Brownsville Echo*, which he renamed the *Prairie County Democrat*. From this platform, he supported Breckinridge, the Democratic candidate for president of the United States. When Abraham Lincoln won the election, and when South Carolina seceded from the United States, Smithee used his newspaper to call for Arkansas also to secede.

Smithee was not content, though, with mere editorial positions. When Little Rock citizens massed with others from Arkansas to take the arsenal out of federal hands, Smithee was part of the group; when Captain James Totten and his 150 soldiers handed the arsenal over to Arkansas in February 1861, Smithee was among those who received it on behalf of the state. In April, he traveled up the Arkansas River with a contingent led by former U.S. senator Solon Borland to claim Fort Smith, which was another quiet success for Arkansas. In May, when Arkansas did secede from the Union and join the Confederate states, Smithee sold his interest in the *Prairie County Democrat* and enlisted in the army. Specifically, he enlisted as a private in the Light Artillery led by William Woodruff Jr., the son of Arkansas's pioneer newspaperman. Through the course of the war, Smithee was promoted several times, ending up as a first lieutenant. By the end of the war, he was an adjutant in W. D. Blocher's artillery battalion.

Smithee's units saw much action during the course of the war, but probably none of it was more distressing to Smithee than the attack upon Helena in July 1863. Although the state capital, Little Rock, would not be captured by Federal forces until September of that year, the Union already had control of much of northern Arkansas following its initial victory at Pea Ridge in 1862. One of the Union's strongholds was Helena, an important port on the Mississippi River. With a major battle looming downstream at Vicksburg, Mississippi, the size of the Federal force at Helena had been reduced, and General Theophilus Holmes hoped that he might strike a blow for the Confederacy by reclaiming Helena. Much of the time,

Confederate strategy had ignored Arkansas, concentrating far more attention on eastern battles than on what it called the Trans-Mississippi Department. Overpowering a Federal stronghold on the Mississippi River, though, might have called attention to the importance of the west in the Civil War and brought more Confederate strength back into Arkansas.

Though the plan had merit, the effort to retake Helena was not pursued effectively. Confederate soldiers outnumbered Federal defenders, but Helena was protected by four artillery batteries strategically located on high ground. General Holmes had hoped to have the advantage of surprise for the battle, but poor communication ruined that. All the commanders were told to advance and attack at sunrise, but some interpreted "sunrise" to mean the first gray light of dawn, while others took it to mean the actual appearance of the sun on the horizon. As a result, the Federal defenders were not surprised by a fierce onslaught, and they were able to hold the city. More than 1,600 Confederate troops were lost, compared to 239 casualties for the Federal defenders. J. N. Smithee was wounded in the battle, which was fought on the very same day that Confederate forces also lost dramatically at Vicksburg and at Gettysburg, Pennsylvania.

After the Civil War, Smithee returned to his journalistic endeavors. He worked briefly as a typesetter in Memphis, but in 1866 he returned to Little Rock, where he was hired as the foreman at the *Arkansas Gazette*'s printing office. His employer was William Woodruff Jr., who had been Smithee's commanding officer during the war. On January 1, 1867, Smithee married Annie E. Cowgill, who was the great-granddaughter of the Benjamin Harrison who signed the Declaration of Independence. During the next several years, Smithee was promoted to city editor and then to managing editor of the *Gazette*, even being made a co-owner of the paper for a time. In 1873, newsmen from around the state of Arkansas met in Little Rock to form a new organization, which they called the Arkansas Press

Association. J. N. Smithee was elected president of the group and served three terms in that office, overseeing its annual gatherings.

In 1872, a political crisis began in Arkansas that would lead to its greatest disruption and violence since the end of the Civil War. Joseph Brooks and Elisha Baxter, both Republicans, fought a spirited campaign to serve as governor of Arkansas. When the votes were counted, Baxter was declared the winner. Brooks and his supporters immediately demanded a recount, pointing out that the men counting the votes were all supporters of Baxter. Brooks appealed to the General Assembly, but it refused to consider his evidence of voting irregularities. Brooks then turned to the courts, which managed to keep his case tied up for over a year while Baxter continued to lead Arkansas as governor.

By early 1874, opinions were changing in Arkansas about Governor Baxter. Among the governor's actions that angered his former supporters was his refusal to sign the paperwork for state bonds that would provide money to build more railroads. A meeting of Republicans, including both U.S. senators from Arkansas, decided to throw their support to Brooks, and Seventh Circuit judge John Whytock agreed to hear his case. On April 15, the judge ruled that Joseph Brooks was indeed the rightfully elected governor of the state. Brooks acted quickly. Taking the county sheriff with him, Brooks and a group of armed men entered the statehouse and forced Baxter to leave immediately.

The deposed governor retreated to St. Johns' College on Ninth Street, where he proceeded to gather his supporters. That evening he led a parade, including most of the students of the college along with 200 other supporters, up the streets of Little Rock to the Anthony House, a hotel near the statehouse which was often used for political meetings. Baxter declared martial law in Arkansas and called upon President Grant to support him. Meanwhile, Brooks barricaded himself in the statehouse and had his supporters gather arms to defend their position. Their weaponry included a cannon that they set up on the statehouse grounds and aimed at the Anthony House.

J. N. Smithee was part of the group supporting Governor Baxter and resisting the attempted overthrow by Joseph Brooks. Baxter designated Smithee a colonel in the state militia, which had grown to about 1,000 men by April 20. Brooks had also assembled a force of about the same size to defend his place in the governor's office. President Grant tried to preserve an appearance of neutrality in the dispute, but he sent orders to Colonel Thomas Rose at the federal arsenal, telling Rose to keep the peace in Arkansas. Rose's federal soldiers took a position on Markham Street between the statehouse and the Anthony House, separating the two sides.

Meanwhile, additional supporters of Baxter and of Brooks continued to pour into Little Rock from all over the state. Many of them were bringing guns and other supplies, anticipating violence. Shots were fired in Little Rock on April 21, resulting in several casualties, and over the next two weeks, fighting broke out in New Gascony (near Pine Bluff), Arkansas Post, Lonoke, and Palarm Creek. Before the fighting ended, more than 200 Arkansans died in what became known as the Brooks-Baxter War. In May, U.S. attorney general George Williams tried to negotiate a settlement with representatives of both sides, suggesting that a special session of the General Assembly should decide the results of the previous election. When Brooks objected to that proposal, President Grant asked Williams to make the decision, which he did on May 15. The attorney general supported Baxter's case, and the next day President Grant promised federal assistance to defend Governor Baxter's right to complete his term of office. Brooks capitulated, surrendered the statehouse, and disbanded his forces. Baxter, who had received much of his political support from Democratic Party figures including Albert Pike and Uriah Rose (as well as J. N. Smithee), led a victory parade to the statehouse on May 19.

Colonel Smithee—apparently as a reward for his support of Governor Baxter—was appointed commissioner of Immigration and State Lands following the conclusion of the Brooks-Baxter War. This job gave Smithee supervision over public works and internal improvements funded by the state, as well as the disposition of tax-delinquent property seized by the state. The new state constitution, written in Little Rock during the summer of 1874 and approved by the voters of the state in October, made the land commissioner an elective office. The same voters chose to keep Smithee as land commissioner the next month; he was reelected to the position in 1876.

Smithee resigned his newspaper positions to pursue his political career, but he appears to have regretted that decision. In April 1878, while he was still land commissioner, Smithee bought the printing equipment of the *Little Rock Star*, which he used to produce a new newspaper, the *Arkansas Democrat*, which began publication on April 11, 1878. Meanwhile, Woodruff had sold the *Arkansas Gazette* to John Adams and William Blocher on November 11, 1876. They had hired James Mitchell to be editor-in-chief of the paper; Mitchell was formerly an English professor at Arkansas Industrial University in Fayetteville, the school that was soon to become the University of Arkansas.

John Adams was in Washington DC much of April 1878, so it was almost certainly Mitchell who first took public notice of the *Democrat*. After remarking, on page two of the April 12 *Gazette*, that the new newspaper would be "a Democratic paper with strong Greenback tendencies," the *Gazette* editor commented that "there is room for another paper in this city—'at the top.' While the *Gazette* does not intend to relinquish its position 'at the top,' we extend a cordial invitation to the new comer to enter the lists, and hope the editor may be more fortunate, financially, than he appears to have been in the office of State Land Commissioner."

Mitchell's reference to "strong Greenback tendencies" highlights one of the major political controversies of the later part of the nineteenth century. U.S. currency was backed, at the time, by the government's gold reserves. Some politicians believed that the currency should be backed by silver rather than by gold (William Jennings Bryan was destined to be the most eloquent defender of that position), while others believed that the value of a dollar should rest on the idea of the dollar itself and not be backed by any precious metal. Smithee's "Greenback tendencies" would not become government policy until the Nixon administration in 1971 ended the gold standard and allowed the dollar to "float."

A more significant difference of opinion between the *Gazette* and the *Democrat* had much more importance to the average politician, business leader, or general newspaper reader in Arkansas, however. The state of Arkansas had fallen into debt before the war because of highly questionable banking practices, and an even larger debt had been assessed to the state of Arkansas because of the Civil War. As a member of the state government and as a newspaper writer, Smithee took the position that Arkansas should repudiate its past debts and make a fresh start, the equivalent of declaring bankruptcy. Writing for the *Gazette*, Mitchell took the opposite opinion, holding to the logic that if Arkansas were to repudiate its past debts for any reason, no one would trust the state government sufficiently to buy bonds in the future to fund the state's projects.

A dignified exchange of opinions about these important issues of the day could have benefited the readers of both papers. Instead, the writers quickly descended into accusations, questioning each other's motives, and engaging in character assassination and downright insults. The *Gazette* published an accusation on April 16 charging that four prominent politicians were paying fifty dollars a month to Smithee and the *Democrat* with the arrangement that the newspaper would keep "a level head between them"—in other words, treat those four in the same way without favoring any of them, while meanwhile feeling free to attack any of their opponents. From that day on, the

Gazette repeatedly demanded to know the names of those four supporters of the *Democrat.* Mitchell also insisted that Smithee was acting unethically, owning and writing for a newspaper while also holding public office in Arkansas.

Smithee, in turn, wrote that the *Gazette* had failed in its duty as a newspaper by refusing to support the state government in its time of need. He even suggested that the principal reason he began the *Democrat* was to challenge the *Gazette* and to support the government of Arkansas. He wrote that the *Gazette* had hidden motives to oppose repudiation of the state debt. On April 22, the *Democrat* said, "It is a well-known fact in financial and official circles that the great majority of our floating indebtedness (State scrip) is held in New York—and it is generally believed Mr. Thompson Dean is one of the largest holders of that scrip, purchased by his partner, Maj. Adams." The *Gazette* quickly denied the charge. On April 27, Smithee complained, "While we expected these differences to result in discussion, we had no idea and did not intend that this dissension should degenerate into personalities, misrepresentations, and abuse."

He had every right to complain of abuse. Among the editorials that were aimed directly and personally at him were such mockeries in the *Gazette* as, "Softly, softly, Jasper Newton. Remember that the weather is warm and that the natural flow of spirits in you makes too much excitement dangerous to your sensitive organization" (April 20) and, "Attempting to 'bust' the *Gazette* is rather a hazardous undertaking. A man named Smith might do us damage, but one named Smithee is too light a weight" (April 28).

Immediately after J. N. Smithee died in 1902—more than twenty years after this debate—the *Gazette* revealed in his obituary that he had challenged James Mitchell to a duel and that Mitchell had accepted the challenge. A duel is far different from a brawl; a duel is fought between two individuals who believe that their honor is at stake and who agree to follow certain rules and procedures in a violent defense of their honor. For this particular duel, Smithee chose R. C. Newton and Robert A. Howard as his "seconds" (witnesses who make sure the rules are followed), and Mitchell chose John N. Moore to fill the same role. Before the day of the duel arrived, however, cooler heads prevailed, and the principals came to an agreement. They composed separate statements "disclaiming any intention on the part of each to reflect upon the honor of the other," promising that both newspapers would print both statements side by side. Smithee published both statements in the *Democrat*, but the essays did not appear in the *Gazette*. One duel had been avoided, but the next would not be.

The reason for the omission on the part of the *Gazette* was that John Adams returned to Little Rock from his trip east. Reading what both newspapers had written during his absence, Adams adopted a different approach, not at all meant to reconcile the writers. On May 2, a letter from Adams to Smithee was published on page one of the *Gazette*. (Mitchell's charges had been less prominent, included among other editorial comments on page two of the paper.) In his letter, Adams described Smithee as a "man who would permit a poor orphan boy (who was learning the printing business) to be discharged for a crime he himself has committed."

Such words led inevitably to the armed confrontation on a Sunday morning in downtown Little Rock that has become known as the last duel fought in Arkansas. Three significant descriptions of the fight give three somewhat different views of what happened. The first, published May 7 in the *Gazette*, says rather tersely that Adams and Smithee met in the streets of Little Rock Sunday morning (May 5), that six or seven shots were fired, and that Smithee was injured twice but Adams was unharmed, although a ball passed through the rim of his hat. Later, in Smithee's obituary in 1902, the *Gazette* reported that Smithee was shot once, "the injury consisting of a flesh wound in the wrist." It also claims that "shortly afterward the old trouble was adjusted, and Smithee, Adams, and Mitchell were ever after good friends."

By far the most colorful description of the duel was published fifty years after it happened, in the memoirs of Opie Read. Read was a young reporter, writing for the *Democrat* at the time of the duel. He went on to a successful career writing humorous essays, often poking gentle fun at his home state. Read's memories of historical events tended to be imaginative and entertaining, even when they were not strictly accurate; yet even as reliable a historian as Michael Dougan of Arkansas State University relies heavily on Read's account to relate the story of the duel of Smithee and Adams in his history of Arkansas newspapers, *Community Diaries*. According to Opie Read, an unusually large Sunday morning crowd was hanging around the streets of Little Rock, anticipating the duel, and preachers firmly tried to pull members of their congregations into their respective church buildings, to no avail. Excitement grew as witnesses saw Smithee and Adams approaching the intersection of Markham and Main streets from different directions. When the duelists saw each other, Read remembered, five shots were fired, and Smithee staggered off the sidewalk and fell into the street. This, according to Read, is when the men cursed each other, with Adams using Smithee's wife and children as his sole excuse not to finish his opponent.

No one can say what effect this public violence had on either newspaper, but both papers were sold to others before the end of the year. Roughly a week after the duel, on May 14, Adams and Blocher sold the *Gazette* to Ambrose Hundley Sevier Jr., son of a pre–Civil War U.S. senator from Arkansas. In October, Blocher and Mitchell purchased the *Democrat* from Smithee.

By this time, Smithee had been named chairman of the Arkansas Democratic Party. In 1880, he sought the office of governor. His principal opponents were incumbent governor William Miller, former Confederate general Thomas Churchill, and William Fishback—who, like Smithee, had a plan to release Arkansas from its burdensome debt. Smithee ran on a platform of economy and reform, which he called the "Young Arkansas" position. In debate before the state's Democratic Party convention, Smithee reminded Fishback and the voters of Fishback's change of heart in 1861, voting against secession before he voted for it. Both of them lost the nomination to Churchill, though, who then easily won the general election.

In a dizzying series of ownership changes, that same year, Don Adams (son of the dueling John Adams) bought the *Gazette* from Ambrose Sevier. On May 4, 1882, Adams sold the *Gazette* to J. N. Smithee. The next month, Smithee invited Major C. G. Newman to be his partner and business manager in the newspaper business. At the beginning of July, the partners announced that they had incorporated the *Gazette*, making Smithee president of the corporation and adding H. G. Allis as secretary. By 1883, Smithee's name no longer appeared in the list of corporation officers; D. A. Brower was now president of the corporation.

In November 1884, Grover Cleveland narrowly won the election for president of the United States, becoming the first Democrat since 1856 to be chosen by the voters as president. The next year, President Cleveland appointed Smithee as a special federal agent of the general land office for the western state of Colorado and territory of New Mexico. Smithee moved to Santa Fe in 1886, and later he moved to Denver, Colorado. In Denver he re-entered the newspaper business, publishing the *Rocky Mountain News* beginning in 1890.

The *Gazette* corporation struggled during the years of Smithee's absence from the state. The newspaper was led by a series of editors, none of whom remained in control for very long. Large amounts of money were lost by the corporation's investors in the Panic of 1893, and *Gazette* secretary H. G. Allis ended up in prison. Jacob Frolich had labor difficulties which caused the unionized printers to walk off the job; Frolich responded by hiring non-union workers from a group that called itself the Printers' Protective Fraternity. Smithee had been a member of the printers' union and is said to have held every position in union leadership, even while he was also owner of various newspapers. When a firm from New York acquired the *Gazette*, Smithee was able to purchase a controlling interest in the paper, and on May 11, 1896, he returned to Little Rock and took control of the *Gazette*. One of his first actions was to reinstate the printers' union and its workers at the newspaper.

During his years in the west, Smithee had changed his convictions from "strong Greenback tendencies" to a strong advocacy of silver. Smithee and the *Gazette* supported the presidential campaigns of silver-backer William Jennings Bryan (who was twice defeated by Republican William McKinley), and Smithee's strongly worded comments about Arkansas politicians drew a fair amount of attention. In 1897, Smithee was visited in the newspaper offices by state senator R. D. McMullen of Yell County. McMullen, who took exception to some recent editorials written by Smithee, drew a gun and fired. Fred Allsopp, an employee of the newspaper who later wrote extensively about the history of Arkansas's newspapers, was standing nearby and was able to jostle McMullen's hand, causing his shot to miss Smithee. Allsopp later remarked, "The editor showed remarkable nerve, never flinching or showing the slightest perturbation." Smithee also chose not to press charges against McMullen.

Smithee pressed a Populist agenda as newspaper editor, suggesting that the role of his newspaper was to tell the truth, leading to the healing of society. Speaking of the *Gazette*, he wrote, "For all her age and experience, the 'Old Lady' may be more of an herb and ointment doctor than diagnostician." He further suggested that the truth must be published "though it tears the hide off our backs." His stubbornness did not endear him to all the political leaders and businessmen of Little Rock, though, and Smithee's last day at the *Gazette* was January 31, 1899. He was replaced as head of the *Gazette* Publishing Company by banker W. B. Worthen.

Smithee had long toyed with the idea of writing a novel, and his leisure time permitted this. The unpublished text of his novel, *Aaron Lewis: A Story of the Southwest*, can be read from microfilm stored at the Arkansas History Commission in Little Rock. So far, no one who has read the text has suggested finding a publisher for it.

Annie and the children remained in Denver, separated from J. N. Smithee, although it does not appear that either husband or wife considered filing for a divorce. Early in 1902, while he was in New York, Smithee slipped and fell on a patch of ice, permanently injuring himself. Returning to Little Rock, he took room number 5 at the Merchants Hotel and continued work on his novel.

A day or two before July 4, J. N. Smithee borrowed a pistol from a friend, claiming that he was being bothered by stray cats at the hotel. No one heard the shot that he fired through his right temple; he appears to have shot himself during the city's fireworks display. His body was found the next day. He left behind three short notes. In one of them, he noted the anniversary of the triple Confederate losses at Helena, Vicksburg, and Gettysburg. In another he declared, "For cripples, paupers, and mendicants I have no use," making clear his motives for the suicide. The third note requested that his body should be cremated, as "all dead bodies should be thus disposed of." Annie and the children did not return to Little Rock for the funeral. Smithee, like many other prominent citizens of Arkansas, is buried at Mount Holly Cemetery.

The suicide took his friends and his opponents by surprise. Fred Allsopp later wrote, "He was a man of commanding personal appearance, generous to a fault, as brave as a lion, possessing strong convictions, and much native ability, but inclined to be somewhat improvident. He was a good newspaper man, who did much for Arkansas. His death was untimely, and a loss to the state."

The *Arkansas Gazette* and *Arkansas Democrat* continued to battle for the patronage of Arkansas's readers for much of the twentieth century. The *Gazette*, which proudly proclaimed itself the oldest paper west of the Mississippi River, won many awards for its news coverage. After it was acquired by the Gannett Corporation in 1986, the *Gazette* lost the confidence of many local readers, and it published its last edition five years later. Its resources were bought by the *Democrat*, and on October 19, 1991, the day after the *Gazette*'s last publication, the first edition of the *Arkansas Democrat-Gazette* rolled off the presses. After more than a century of competition, the *Democrat* had finally assured itself of a place "at the top."

V.

Sid Wallace:
Outlaw, Avenger, or Scapegoat?

The Civil War and its aftermath delivered hard times to Arkansas. These hard times brought out the best in some Arkansans, but other residents of the state seem to have responded with their worst instincts and behavior. Armed bands of ruffians roamed the countryside, not aligned with Federal or Confederate forces, but merely robbing and threatening violence for their own purposes. Feuds between families simmered for years, occasionally erupting into gunfire that left men dead in the streets. The end of the war did not mean an end to the lawlessness; Arkansas was a frontier state, and many parts of Arkansas resembled the Old West more than they did the world of the southern plantation. The Ku Klux Klan arose, ostensibly to bring vigilante justice, but in truth to promote intolerance through fear and violence. Governor Powell Clayton was forced to declare martial law in fourteen Arkansas counties in 1868, three years after the war presumably had ended.

The story of Sid Wallace is woven into that fabric of lawlessness and violence in Arkansas's Reconstruction period. Sid's execution for murder was noted even in the *New York Times* as just retribution for a life of crime. Later writers would use Sid's story to represent the desperate need for law and order in Arkansas and in the neighboring Indian Territory which would become the state of Oklahoma. Not all writers condemn Sid as a common criminal, though. Some hint that Sid was a local hero, resisting the carpetbaggers who came to the South after the war to profit from its decline. They see Sid as also punishing the scalawags of Arkansas who cooperated with these northern profiteers. Sid's status as a folk hero, though not as widely published, puts him in the category of post-war outlaws such as Jesse James and Belle Starr. Sid Wallace may have contributed deliberately to that legend before he died, but he did not embrace it fully. He insisted that he had never killed a man except in self-defense, and he told reporters that he had been framed and was being put to death for crimes committed by others.

Sidney Wallace was born on August 11, 1851, on the Wallace family farm near Clarksville, Arkansas, the county seat of Johnson County. Johnson County is in the Arkansas River Valley, downstream from Fort Smith but upriver from Little Rock. In addition to farmland, the county also boasts of peach orchards, coal mines, and rich forest lands. Sid was the fifth of seven children born to Vincent Wallace and Ruth Suggs Wallace; Vincent, in addition to farming, was a Methodist minister who had been elected to the Arkansas House of Representatives in 1852. Some writers claim that Vincent joined the Confederate troops from Johnson County at the start of the Civil War, then was sent home by his unit so he could help keep order back home with so many men gone from the area. Vincent's name, however, is not included in any official records of Confederate soldiers from Arkansas.

Following the battles at Pea Ridge and Prairie Grove, northwest Arkansas was convincingly held by the Union. No significant military engagements took place in Johnson County. The Federal army retained some units to hold Fort Smith and Fayetteville while it sent other forces to capture Helena, Arkansas Post, and finally Little Rock. Clarksville suffered during the occupation, though, when a Federal regiment came through the city. The Federals claimed the Presbyterian Church as a hospital, then burned it to the ground as they left the city. The county jail and the Methodist church were also destroyed, and the courthouse was damaged. Though Johnson County had not been solidly behind secession when the question first was raised—and some men from the county fought for the Union while others fought for the Confederacy—the lasting impression in 1865 was that Federal soldiers had not been good for Johnson County.

On the last day of 1863, Vincent Wallace was accosted outside his farmhouse by three men wearing Union army coats. No record of the conversation exists, so speculation abounds. They may have been common thieves demanding plunder from the farm. They may have been making more specific demands. One writer speculates that the preacher knew the location of the estranged girlfriend of one of his assailants but protected her by withholding that information from his visitors. No one can be certain even whether the attackers were Federal soldiers or were bushwhackers using the coats as a disguise. What is known is that Vincent Wallace was fatally shot on December 31, 1863. Several accounts add the detail that the three men also shot the family dog and dropped its body into the well.

Sid Wallace may have been a witness to his father's murder. Most writers say that he was sheltered from the sight by Missouri Blackard, often called "Aunt Missouri." She was an African American woman who had been a slave of the Wallace family. According to President Lincoln's Emancipation Proclamation, Blackard had been free from slavery for an entire year, ever since January 1. Not only was she still with the Wallace family on the day of Vincent's murder, but she continued to work for them for many years, even long after the war had ended. Nearly every writer who describes the killing insists on the following: Blackard recognized all three of the attackers, but she refused to tell Sid their names. Instead, she kept their identities secret until Sid's twenty-first birthday, when he would be mature enough to seek revenge.

A curiously mixed picture of the young Sid Wallace has been created by his biographers. On the one hand, he is invariably described as a handsome man, attracting much attention from all the young ladies of Johnson County. On the other hand, he is frequently described as a gloomy, brooding figure, frightening the parents of those same young ladies with his menacing gaze, violence clearly lurking under the surface. This complex portrayal may be more than the invention of later writers. The legend of Sid Wallace as lady-charmer and dangerous criminal already appears in newspapers in the weeks before Sid's execution.

One report, written nearly a century after the event, describes Sid Wallace traveling to Kansas to exact his revenge upon his father's murderers. Presumably, Missouri Blackard kept her promise to tell Sid the names of his father's three killers on his twenty-first birthday, or perhaps a year or more earlier. How Sid learned that one of the killers had relocated to Kansas is never explained, but the account describes him traveling to Kansas, finding the murderer, and staying the night with him and his family, claiming to be a peddler. He even displayed his wares to the family to make his story convincing. Only in the morning, as he was taking leave of the family, did he identify himself as the son of Vincent Wallace, as he drew a pistol and shot his host dead. No charges were ever filed against Sid for this cold-blooded act, nor was it mentioned during his trials for the killings that happened in Johnson County.

In May 1871—several weeks before Sid's twentieth birthday—two Johnson County men were attacked on the road to Clarksville. Joseph T. Dickey was a "drummer" (a traveling salesman) and Dud Turner was his friend. Their attackers were two men on horseback who covered their faces with bandanas. The incident seems no more than a typical highway robbery and was reported as such at the time. One of the robbers fired a gun, injuring Dickey, but Turner was able to flee with his injured friend into Clarksville, where Dickey received treatment and recovered from the wound. Turner told everyone who would listen that the robbers were "those Wallace boys," and he insisted that Sid was the gunman who had wounded Dickey. Later writers identified Dickey as the second of Vincent Wallace's murderers, but they also misidentify Dickey as a foreman for the railroad that was then being built through Clarksville to connect Little Rock and Fort Smith. They err further by saying that Dickey died of his wounds.

Sid Wallace was arrested for the attack on the strength of Dud Turner's eyewitness account. (Wallace would later claim to have been at home with his brothers at the time of the attack on Dickey and Turner.) The county jail, destroyed during the war, had not yet been rebuilt, and Sid was held in a second-floor room of the Hershey building in downtown Clarksville. Sid had no difficulty removing the window and dropping onto the roof of an adjacent shed, thus escaping his confinement. Turner left town around that time, apparently relocating to Indian Territory. No further attempt was made to hold Sid and his brother accountable for the crime until late in 1873.

In January 1873, Dud Turner returned to Clarksville. Sid and George Wallace found him in town and sought revenge for the accusations he had filed against them. According to newspaper reports, Sid aimed a gun at Turner while George beat him viciously, badly wounding him. Shortly thereafter, Turner evened the score by shooting George to death; he then escaped a second time to Indian Territory. Around that time, a man remembered only as "old man Davis" was shot and killed in Clarksville. Even at the time, Sid Wallace was accused of the murder, although no charges were ever filed against him for that crime. Later writers accepted the rumor that Sid had shot Mr. Davis, explaining that Davis was another of the men who had killed Sid's father in 1863. If this assumption is correct, then in early 1873 Sid was back in the revenge business after a vacation of roughly a year and a half.

One of the most interesting incidents in the legend of Sid Wallace is frequently placed at this point in his biography—early 1873—although other writers prefer to report the event as occurring in September or October of 1873. According to several accounts, a group of men set out for the Wallace house to arrest Sid, but none of them had the courage to approach the house and demand his surrender. Fearing the results of a potential shoot-out with the desperate criminal, the posse chose instead to surround the house, preventing his escape, hoping for a peaceful arrest at the conclusion of their siege. All remained quiet for the rest of the day. Then, as night fell, Missouri Blackard left the house, carrying a bucket to the well, her voluminous skirt attracting no attention from the watching men. Hiding under the skirt of "Aunt Missouri" was Sid Wallace. In the darkness, as she filled her bucket at the well, he slipped away from her; the first warning of his escape to reach the ears of his pursuers was the sound of his horse galloping away in the nighttime.

Clarksville remained quiet for the rest of the spring and the first part of the summer, but the peaceful community was shattered by a pair of murders in the last days of August 1873. Constable R. W. "Doc" Ward was the first victim to be assassinated. Doc Ward had first come to Arkansas with the Federal army during the Civil War; like some other northern soldiers, Ward had stayed in the South after the war to make his fortune. Such men often were described as "carpetbaggers," suggesting that their only motivation to remain in the South was to profit at the expense of the defeated and demoralized southerners. Carpetbaggers had rebuilt the government of Arkansas and other southern states, even representing these states in the U.S. House of Representatives and Senate, as well as in state legislatures and in governors' offices. Carpetbaggers had opened banks, built railroads, started businesses, and constructed houses for themselves and their families. Many carpetbaggers, like Doc Ward, had been appointed or elected to positions of local authority. Ward does not appear to have been generally disliked in Johnson County; he was just a man doing his job, like so many other men around the county. Still, as constable, he had a responsibility to arrest criminals, and anyone pursuing a life of crime could expect to profit from the elimination of the local enforcer of the law.

Doc Ward was sitting on a wooden sidewalk in front of W. P. Rose's drugstore one fine summer evening—August 20, 1873—when a single gunshot rang out, and the constable fell, mortally wounded. He did not die until September 12, however. The shocked witnesses reported that a gunman had fired a double-barreled shotgun at the constable and then ridden away on horseback. No one was arrested for the crime. Exactly one week later, county judge Elisha Mears was walking home for his noontime meal after a pleasant visit to Blind Bob's Saloon in Clarksville when, once again, a single shot rang out. Mears fell, badly injured—he died an hour after midnight. Witnesses said that the gunman had been concealed, but no one claimed to know who had fired the shots. Tongues began to wag, though, and fingers of blame were being pointed at Sid Wallace. Even in Little Rock, the *Arkansas Gazette* took notice of the crimes, grumbling that no effort was being made to bring the assassin to justice. Citizens of Johnson County were not as blind to criminal behavior, however, as the Little Rock journalist suggested. More than a century later, one writer would characterize their attitude with these words: "The killing of Judge Meers [sic], a progressive Johnson County native, turned the tide of public opinion in Clarksville against Sid Wallace. Sid was the prime suspect, and most thought he should not have shot the judge, even if he was a Republican."

The situation was, of course, more complicated than the quip suggests. Government officials were being shot down in the streets of the county seat. These shootings were taking place during Reconstruction, an era when some citizens maintained their Confederate sympathies and resented any official, whether northern-born or native, who cooperated with the Republican government officials who had taken charge in Arkansas after the war. Moreover, law enforcement had become a problem in many parts of Arkansas. The guerrilla bands that had terrorized the population during the war, whether bushwhackers or jayhawkers, did not automatically disband when the war ended. Family feuds and local conflicts simmered periodically into violence in all parts of Arkansas. The Pope County Militia War, not far from Johnson County, broke out in 1865 and 1866. Soldiers sent from Little Rock kept the peace for a time, but after they left, more violence flared again in 1872 and 1873. The city of Waldron, in Scott County, had similar bouts of violence in the 1870s. In Monroe County, James Hind—a member of the U.S. House of Representatives from Arkansas—was assassinated in 1868. Surrounded by all this violence, if the Wallace brothers had chosen a life of crime resembling that of the more famous James brothers of Missouri, few would be overly surprised, though most would not approve. During these tumultuous times, few would also be surprised if any citizen chose to overthrow the local government by means of a few well-aimed gunshots.

Sid Wallace could not be arrested, though, merely on the basis of gossip and a bad reputation. Dud Turner was out of town, and at first no eyewitness was available to report on the shooter who had struck down Ward and Mears. In time, though, a witness was produced. Thomas Paine reported to authorities that he had come upon Sid Wallace hiding in a position of ambush two days before the shooting of the constable. Paine even said that Sid had promised to get rid of the constable. Armed with this key bit of information, authorities gathered and placed Sid under arrest.

The arrest did not happen, though, in Johnson County. Instead, Sid was seized in Lewisburg, more than fifty miles away. The arrest was made on October 16 by Polk Allnutt, the marshal of Lewisburg, and Sheriff Stout of Conway County. Sid was returned to Clarksville, where he was carefully watched until his trials, conviction, and sentencing.

His two trials began on November 11. On November 14 he was convicted of the attack on Dickey and Turner and sentenced to serve four years in the state penitentiary. Evidence was then considered regarding the assassination of the constable. On November 24, Sidney Wallace was convicted of the murder of Constable Doc Ward and was sentenced to be hanged until dead. He was never tried for the murder of Judge Mears, nor for any of the other violent crimes of which he had been accused.

Until his conviction and sentencing, Sid evidently did not contemplate any daring escape (although some writers identify his adventure involving the skirts of Missouri Blackard with the arrest of Wallace that autumn). Sid appears to have believed that his defense was based on a solid alibi: he could not have shot Ward and Mears because he was sick in bed at the time of both shootings, suffering from the measles. Both his mother and the servant, Blackard, testified about his illness. The same evidence would later be produced when the case was appealed, but no one, it seems, believed that a case of measles had disabled the bold outlaw.

Of course, given his history of successful escapes, Sid was carefully watched in the improvised county jail on the second floor of the Hershey building. County officials were determined that Sid would not be permitted to slip out a window a second time. As evidence of their vigilance, no further proof is needed than the fact that two armed guards were present on the day when Sid's younger brothers, Matt and Tom, visited him at the jail. (Telling the story to a reporter later, Sid remembered six guards, but most sources mention only two.) These guards are remembered largely for their failure in their duties. Catching them unawares during his brothers' visit, Sid managed to seize the rifle of one of the guards. The other guard dropped his gun, and both fled the building. The occasion for this daring move was not another attempt at escape. From his second-floor window, Sid had seen Thomas Paine, the witness whose testimony had led to Sid's conviction. Sid

this incarceration as well. According to legend, Sid Wallace quickly attracted the attention of the daughter of the penitentiary warden. So besotted was she that she begged her father's permission to permit the handsome prisoner to escort her to a dance being held in Little Rock. Surprisingly, he agreed. Not surprisingly, when she next asked, after the dance, if her father would allow Sid to escape the penitentiary so the young couple could elope, he refused and allowed no further contact between his daughter and the prisoner.

This charming romance is marred by a lack of recorded names for the generous warden and his impressionable daughter. One writer calls the warden the superintendent of the state prison, but Superintendent H. B. Robinson was responsible for the administration of the prison. He would not have visited it often, and would not have allowed his daughter on the premises. A more likely candidate for the nameless warden is James M. Peck. Peck had signed a contract with the State of Arkansas to lease prisoners from the penitentiary for work of various kinds around the state. Prisons were expensive then as now, and the State of Arkansas was trying to reduce the costs of incarceration and even generate a profit through this convict-lease system. Criminals were rented from the state to work in cotton fields and coal mines and other forms of hard labor; convicts would even be employed to build the new state capitol on the grounds of the old penitentiary. Minimum standards were set governing the food and clothing and healthcare provided to leased convicts. Sid might possibly have been rented for the night to Peck as an escort for his lovely daughter; but, alas, census records indicate that Peck had no wife or sons or daughters at the time when Sid Wallace was in prison.

Another writer claims that, while in the state penitentiary, Sid once seized a gun from one of his guards. Some local visitors to the prison, seeing the situation, calmly told Sid that even if he shot the guard and the visitors, he would still be locked in a prison cell with no means of escape. With a smile, Sid acknowledged the truth of their statement and returned the gun to his guard.

Whatever other stories might be created about Sid's weeks in Little Rock, he did at least have the privilege of several interviews with local reporters. At this time, he insisted to them that his appeal would succeed. Sid affirmed to the press that he had never shot a man except in self-defense, and he repeated that he had been sick in bed at the time of the murders of Doc Ward and Judge Mears. Sid told the papers that powerful men in Johnson County were behind the shootings and that they had framed Sid for the murders because they knew that their lies would be believed. "Money convicted me," Sid told one reporter on December 15. "The only hope I have is the [Arkansas] Supreme Court. … They can't buy the Supreme Court." Sid's appeal was based largely on the assertion that he could not have a fair trial in Johnson County because of these powerful men who had framed him.

Sid also complained that his life had been ruined by these false accusations. He described his arrest after the attack on Dickey and Turner and his escape through the second-floor window. He then said that he was laid up for a month at home because of a foot injury and that guards surrounded the family home during that entire month. (Perhaps this month-long vigil planted the seed of the story about the nervous posse that would not enter the Wallace house and about Sid's escape under the skirts of "Aunt Missouri.") "They won't let me have a fair trial," Sid complained. He was taken, heavily guarded, back to Clarksville for his hanging on December 18, but at the last minute, Judge Elhanan Searle of the Arkansas Supreme Court granted a stay so the court could consider Sid's appeal. The court agreed to hear his case early in the new year.

The case against Sid Wallace is difficult to assess after the passage of so many years. He was convicted of an attack on Joseph Dickey based on the testimony of Dud Turner, and he was convicted of the murder of Doc Ward based on the testimony of Thomas Paine. Neither is around today to be cross-examined, Turner having fled the county (and undoubtedly having died by this time) and Paine having been shot dead by Sid Wallace. Sid's dire words about a conspiracy of powerful men in Johnson County framing him to hide their own guilt might be heard more sympathetically today than they were at the time he spoke them. Aside from Sid Wallace assertions, though, no one has ever offered proof of such a conspiracy.

The Arkansas Supreme Court clearly was unconvinced by Sid's arguments. The court ruled against his appeal on February 5, 1874. Sid continued to be held in Little Rock until March 9, with the date for his hanging finally scheduled for March 14. On March 10, the *Arkansas Gazette* reported that 1,068 Johnson County residents had signed a petition requesting that Wallace's sentence be commuted. No response was given to this petition.

By this time, the newspapers in Arkansas (led by the *Arkansas Gazette*) had made Sid Wallace a celebrity. Both before and after his appeal was denied, reporters interviewed him in his cell, and their accounts of conversations they had with Sid received considerable space in the newspapers. Sid's execution was guaranteed to be a popular event. Several newspapers sent correspondents to cover the hanging. Every detail about Sid that could be reported was reported: the history of the crimes of which he was accused, the nature of his defense, and even his state of mind about the trials and about the coming execution.

If later writers can be believed, though, the *Gazette* missed one of the biggest stories connected to the execution. C. H. McKennon wrote a book in 1967 about the U.S. marshals in Arkansas and in the Indian Territory at the end of the nineteenth century. In this book, *Iron Men*, McKennon tells with great relish the legend of Sid Wallace, including the murder of his father (identifying the murderers as members of Company C of the 2nd Kansas Regiment), Sid's vow of revenge, his trip to Kansas, his escape under the skirts of Aunt Missouri, and even his illicit romance with the warden's daughter in Little Rock. McKennon uses Sid Wallace as a case study to demonstrate the need for better law enforcement on the frontier, a need which was answered by the marshals who came to Arkansas.

McKennon describes the concern of Clarksville's new marshal, Bud McConnell, that Sid might have accomplices preparing to rescue him from hanging by means of a daring train robbery that would snatch Sid from the hands of the law. Determined to prevent such an escape, McConnell himself seized the train and demanded an unscheduled Sunday trip to Little Rock and back, bringing Sid to Clarksville a day early to foil his would-be rescuers. Heavily armed, McConnell and his deputies are described as watching Sid carefully every mile of the way, while shocked citizens stared with amazement at the rare Sunday run of the train. McConnell's plan succeeded, and Sid was brought to Clarksville and placed in the newly completed county jail.

The *Gazette* merely reports that Sid Wallace arrived uneventfully in Clarksville on Tuesday, March 10. Subsequent articles mentioned the hundreds of spectators who came to the city from all over Johnson County and beyond to witness the hanging. Sid remained defiant to the end. The night before the hanging, he told a reporter, "These fellows are all afraid of me, and for that reason they are going to kill me. How I would love to die fighting. … If I was loose and had a six-shooter, I think I could send the boys off mightily."

A front-page article on March 15 vividly describes the execution, which had taken place the day before as scheduled. According to the *Gazette*, a doctor examined the hanging body after twenty-five minutes and reported that Sid's heart was still beating. Therefore, the corpse was allowed to dangle at the end of the rope for another fifteen minutes before Sid was pronounced dead and removed for burial.

Though this execution with its careful medical examination was witnessed by hundreds of people, rumors persist to this day that Sid Wallace did not die at that time. Some Johnson County residents have heard from their forefathers that the coffin placed in Sid's cemetery plot contained only sand, not his body. The Wallace family moved out of the Clarksville area shortly after the execution, and some people whisper that they did so to hide the fact that Sid remained alive.

Clearly, many elements of his legend could only have developed years after Sid Wallace died. No one who was there on March 14, 1874, could have doubted that Sid really had died. Yet some elements of Sid's legend were already emerging on that day. Among the details reported by the *Gazette* are these curious features. A Little Rock woman sent Sid a bouquet of flowers and a basket of fruit, accompanied by a mysterious note. Sid's last message to his mother, according to the *Gazette*, was a note that said, "Ma, tell all the neighbor girls to drop a bunch of flowers in my coffin, and take the boquet [sic] that the young lady sent me from Little Rock and drop it in my coffin. The box of fruit the same girl sent me, keep it for her sake and memory. Sid." So, the dangerous criminal who fascinated the ladies actually did exist in 1874.

On the other hand, Sid's trail of vengeance as he hunted down the killers of his father seems very likely to be a later creation. Nothing Sid said to reporters from his prison cell suggests such a motive for his crimes, nor did anyone associated with Sid ever suggest that idea. More likely, as twentieth-century Arkansans looked back to the struggles of Reconstruction, they hungered for a hero who took a stand against the carpetbaggers and scalawags who had taken advantage of Arkansas and her sister states during their darkest hours. Young, violent Sid Wallace came close to fitting the pattern they were seeking. Even his claim that he never killed a man except in self-defense can make Sid appear more the hero than the criminal type. The tragic death of Sid's father suggests the rest of the story.

If, on the other hand, Sid is nothing more than a preacher's son turned bad, a common criminal of the lawless West, he is no less interesting today. Even if McKennon pads his account of Sid Wallace's brief life with rumor and with fantasy, he still makes the clear point that firmer and better-trained law enforcement was needed in Arkansas and nearby regions at the time. Sid may have dreamed of the glamorous life of a western outlaw; others may have feared the consequences of such a dream. Even the *New York Times* was prepared, in the month of Sid's death, to express that fear. After giving a slightly garbled account of the alleged crimes of Sidney Wallace, the *Times* mournfully reported that Sidney's mother "seems to have rather gloried in his crimes than condemned them." It adds that "she would do her utmost to induce his brothers to follow in his footsteps." The *Times* then moralizes, "It would be difficult to imagine anything more shocking than this, and it is to be hoped that the feeling which we are told now animates the advocates of law and order in Arkansas will make the exhibition of such blood-thirstiness on the part of an educated woman impossible in the future."

If the *Times*'s sources are correct about the words of Ruth Wallace, perhaps the *Times* misunderstood what she meant by those words. After all, she had continuously supported Sid's alibi, saying under oath that he had been bed-bound with measles at the time of the murders of Doc Ward and Judge Mears. After Sid's conviction, Ruth worked tirelessly to have a higher court review the evidence with the hope that the decision of the jury would be reversed. Instead of endorsing a life of crime, she very likely agreed with her son that he was the victim of powerful men who were framing Sid for crimes he had never committed.

Sid Wallace could be many different things. He could be, as he and his mother claimed, a victim sacrificed to protect others. He could be, as the *Times* reported, a frightening example of the need for law and order. He could be, as others have suggested, a local hero defending the South even after the end of the Civil War as he sought revenge for the wartime murder of his father. Clearly, Sid Wallace was a troubled young man, living in troubled times. Stripped of embellishment, his story remains a vivid picture of the nature of Arkansas during the troubled times of Reconstruction.

VI.

Scipio Africanus Jones:
Black Attorney in a White Man's World

Scipio Jones was born during the Civil War, and he died eighty years later during the Second World War. Those eighty years saw dramatic changes in the way people lived in Arkansas, especially in the way African American people lived in Arkansas. Jones was one of the few African Americans who was able to enjoy a professional career, political power, and comfort bordering on luxury during this time. He owned several nice houses in Little Rock and had a chauffer-driven automobile. During the civil rights movement that reshaped the United States, including Arkansas, in the thirty years following World War II, some people looked back at Scipio Jones and his peers with scorn, suggesting that Jones and others made life worse for their fellow blacks, cooperating with the corrupt system planned by whites who benefited from that system. A different look at the life and career of Scipio Jones reveals that Jones did use his position in Arkansas to help his fellow blacks, challenging the legal and social system that was designed to help white people and hinder the advancement of black people. Whether Jones did everything he could to fight the system can be debated, but the record clearly shows that Jones did battle to change the system even if he also profited from that same system that was so harmful to other men and women like him.

The exact date when Scipio Africanus Jones was born is unknown, although most researchers place his birth in or near August 1863. His mother, Jemmima Jones, was an African American slave, as was her husband, Horace Jones. Scipio, however, was repeatedly recorded in U.S. censuses as "mulatto." This term was used by the U.S. government, and in general usage, to describe a person of mixed European and African ancestry. More recently, the word has declined in usage because of its offensive suggestion of the word "mule," an animal descended from a horse and a donkey. Other parts of the South had a more specific vocabulary for mixed ancestry, including "quadroon"—a person with three white grandparents and one black grandparent—and "octoroon"—a person with seven white great-grandparents and one black great-grandparent. Such terms were not generally used in Arkansas, where common assumptions—and even a law passed by the state's General Assembly in 1911—stated that anyone with a black ancestor was black.

This statement, often called the "one-drop rule," was very significant during Scipio's lifetime, when laws segregated whites and blacks in many ways. White children and black children could not attend the same school. White people and black people could not ride in the same car of a train. Businesses and even public drinking fountains were often labeled "white" or "colored." The Scott Plantation Settlement in Lonoke County, Arkansas, has preserved a building that was once a medical clinic. It had two entrances and two waiting rooms, one for white patients and one for black patients, even though the same doctor saw all the same patients and presumably used the same instruments on all of them when treating them in the same examining room beyond the waiting rooms. Whole cities were designed and built, including West Helena in Phillips County (eastern Arkansas) and Huttig in Union County (southern Arkansas), to have white neighborhoods and black neighborhoods, each with their own homes and businesses and churches and schools, so that the residents of the two sides of the community would never even cross paths. Other towns and cities, especially in northern Arkansas, simply restricted themselves to white residents, telling any black traveler that he or she must be out of town by sundown.

These restrictive rules, which have come to be known as "Jim Crow laws," were deliberately designed to keep white people apart from black people. Some people of mixed ancestry had pale skin and few other African features of hair and face. They managed to "pass"—meaning that they lived among white people as if they were white. They claimed to be white and received the privileges that white people claimed for themselves. On occasion, a fictitious Indian ancestor (for some reason, frequently a "Cherokee princess") was invented to explain away non-European traits in the appearance of someone who was trying to "pass." Cherokee ancestors were socially acceptable during the Jim Crow time, but African ancestors were not acceptable.

The idea of different human races, or of "white blood" and "black blood," continues into the modern day to frame the views some people have of themselves and their neighbors. Scientific studies, including examination of human DNA, however, have largely discredited these views. Differences in DNA that carry racial traits, including skin color and hair texture, are more slight than differences in DNA that exist between two children of the same parents. Moreover, to add some perspective to this issue, nearly all people living in North America today will find ancestors from several parts of the world if they research their family tree back several generations.

Horace Jones was the legal father of Scipio Jones, but clearly a white man was Scipio's biological father. Researchers, almost without exception, identify Sanford Reamey, the plantation owner who also owned Horace and Jemmima Jones, as the father of Scipio Jones. The interest he took in Scipio's education and career is strong evidence of his paternity, even if their relationship was never formally declared. Reamey had acquired ownership of Horace and Jemmima, along with eighteen other slaves, when a relative of Reamey, Dr. Adolphus Jones, died in 1858, and Reamey became the guardian of nine-year-old Theresa Jones, Adolphus's daughter. When the slaves became free and were invited to choose a last name, it is interesting that they chose the name of their previous owner, Jones, rather than the name of their most recent owner, Reamey. It is also interesting that a baby, born to a slave in 1863, should somehow be given the names "Scipio Africanus," remembering the Roman general who won his nickname Africanus by leading his legions into victory against the city of Carthage back in the days of the Roman Republic. Even Scipio's name reflects the interest of an educated man.

Reamey's plantations were in Dallas County in south-central Arkansas. Around the time that Scipio was born, the Federal army was advancing on Little Rock, and many Arkansans were planning to flee to safer territory. Reamey moved his family and his slaves to Texas during the war. When they returned to Arkansas, he employed many of the freed slaves in the same cotton fields where they had labored for him before the war. Scipio worked in the fields with the others, but he also attended elementary schools in the area of Tulip, Arkansas. That settlement, which before the war had been a prominent feature of Dallas County, with more than one famous academy, was already beginning a decline into oblivion that would be completed when it was bypassed by the railroads. The schools Scipio attended were built and maintained only for black children, but they gave him a good enough education (perhaps reinforced by Mr. Reamey's tutoring) that he could read and write by the age of eight and was successful in higher education at an early age.

Thomas Jefferson (himself a slave-owner) had written in the Declaration of Independence in 1776 that "all men are created equal, that they are endowed by their Creator with certain inalienable rights, that among these are life, liberty, and the pursuit of happiness." Following the Civil War, three amendments were added to the U.S.

Constitution to guarantee and defend that equality, particularly in the case of the former slaves. After the original fervor of Reconstruction, however, the U.S. Supreme Court compromised that promise of equality by permitting a state or community to offer "separate but equal" facilities and opportunities for white and black citizens. This ruling made possible the segregation that Scipio Jones knew all his life. One method that cities and counties used to follow the letter of the "separate but equal" ruling without sticking to the spirit of its intention was to separate tax money by families. Taxes paid by white families supported white schools, and taxes paid by black families supported black schools. Even in places where black children far outnumbered white children, the poverty of the black families meant that little money would be available for a school building, a teacher, or any educational materials. The white children had a larger and nicer building, a better paid and better prepared teacher, and more plentiful educational materials.

Because of the interest of his sponsor and presumed father, Sanford Reamey, Scipio Jones was able to rise above the limits of this system. While he was in his teens, Scipio moved to Little Rock and took college preparatory classes at Walden Seminary (which later became Philander Smith College), completing a four-year program in only three years. He then attended Bethel Institute (now Shorter College) in North Little Rock, earning a bachelor's degree in 1885. During these years, Scipio worked a number of part-time jobs around Little Rock to meet his expenses. These jobs included farm labor near the city on the property of James Lawson. With his degree, Jones became a school teacher in Sweet Home, a settlement on the south end of Little Rock. In addition to teaching, Scipio continued his studies, focusing on a career in law. Once again, the mentoring of Reamey benefited Scipio Jones, as several prominent white lawyers in Little Rock guided his studies. On June 15, 1889, Jones passed the bar exam, which meant that he was entitled to serve as a lawyer in the state of Arkansas. His credentials were accepted by the Supreme

Court of Arkansas in 1900 and by the U.S. Supreme Court in 1905. Most of the black lawyers in Arkansas at that time had trained at northern schools such as the University of Chicago or the Boston College School of Law. Even so, only twenty-seven black lawyers were admitted to the Arkansas bar between 1891 and 1923, the years following Scipio's acceptance. Scipio Jones was exceptional in being a "home-grown" Arkansas lawyer of African American descent.

He also was exceptional as a trial lawyer. Most black attorneys in Arkansas prepared contracts, arranged adoptions, helped to write wills, and did other kinds of office work. Black clients who needed a lawyer and could afford one generally preferred a white lawyer. White clients also chose a white lawyer most of the time. Generally, a black lawyer would speak in court only if he were appointed by the court to represent an indigent client. Jones did not match this pattern; he appeared before the Arkansas Supreme Court and in federal district court forty-five times between 1891 and his death in 1943.

Some later writers have suggested that Jones succeeded largely because he "played the game," allowing white people to take advantage of him and of other African Americans so he could profit from a system that was stacked against most of his fellow blacks. Even writers sympathetic to Jones make statements that suggest such compromises. His good friend, a white lawyer named J. H. Carmichael, who became dean of the Arkansas Law School, said of Jones, "In his appearances at court, he always conducted himself in such a way as not to offend the sensibilities of the white jurors, the white judges, and the white attorneys." Historian Grif Stockley has written that Jones and his colleagues "found the most sympathetic white men with power and cultivated them assiduously." Jones reportedly defended one African American client by saying to the jurors, "Now white folks—this is just a poor old nigger boy—he didn't mean any harm."

The most famous legal case involving Scipio Jones is that of the Elaine Massacre of 1919. This notorious event was triggered by an effort to unionize the farm workers of eastern Arkansas. When people today think of the labor movement and labor unions, many think first of factory workers, then perhaps of miners or truck drivers. In the nineteenth century, however, agricultural workers were also creating unions to try to create better working conditions for themselves. Many farm workers at this time, especially on the old cotton plantations, were tenant farmers. They lived on the plantations and worked in the fields for a share of the profit of the farms. The owners of the land set the price of the cotton that was harvested. Many of the owners also monopolized the only stores where tenant farmers could purchase groceries and other necessary goods for their homes and families. Under this system, tenant farmers—both white and black—were kept mired in poverty, always in debt to the owners of the land, unable to raise enough money through their work to escape the farms and find a better life for themselves or for their children.

As miners and factory workers elsewhere were organizing to fight for more freedom and more control of their lives and careers, so also farm workers were organizing into unions. Political movements responded to these unions, promising to reshape the laws to provide the freedom that farm workers craved. A few union movements united the concerns of white farm workers and black farm workers. More often, in states like Arkansas, a union would provide separate chapters in the same town or county, one for white workers and one for black workers. Black or white, though, the workers wanted the same thing: higher prices per pound for cotton, along with other freedoms that would give them more control over their lives and careers rather than tying them and their children to farms they never could own.

The Progressive Farmers and Household Union was meeting in a small church building in Hoop Spur, an unincorporated town near Elaine, Arkansas, on the night of September 30, 1919. An African American group of farmers attended the meeting to learn how they could organize for better cotton prices and more freedom for themselves and their families. Sensing the likelihood of trouble, the union had posted armed guards around the building to protect the meeting from interference. After midnight, an armed group of whites, led by deputy sheriff Charles Pratt, approached the building, purportedly as law enforcement officers. Shots were exchanged; no one knows who fired first. The shoot-out spread to the surrounding area, and quickly—amazingly quickly—word was spread around eastern Arkansas that the blacks of Phillips County were staging an armed revolt against the government. More whites took up arms, and during the first four days of October, the battle continued. Vigilantes from Mississippi and Tennessee joined Arkansans to oppose the alleged uprising of the blacks, and Arkansas governor Charles Hillman Brough even sent in troops from Little Rock, armed with twelve machine guns as well as more conventional firearms, to restore order in Elaine and Phillips County.

To this day, people can be found in Phillips County who believe that the blacks were indeed planning an armed revolt to murder white landowners and seize their farms, while also executing county leaders and law enforcement officials. Those who have studied the Elaine Massacre have concluded that this rumor drew whites with guns into the conflict, but that no such plot was being considered. For example, Grif Stockley writes, "One must keep in mind that there was no black insurrection at Elaine. ... The story of a planned insurrection was concocted on October 2 by the white power structure in Phillips County in order to legitimate the actions of white mobs the previous day." In the end, the numbers speak for themselves. In four days of shooting, five white citizens died. Four were members of the Phillips County law enforcement team, or members of the posse led by that team. The fifth was a soldier from Camp Pike, one of the 538 sent to the county by Governor Brough. Estimates of the number of black citizens who died range from as few as twenty to as many as eight hundred, but generally suggest a number closer to three hundred. In the aftermath of the deaths, 143 men were arrested. All were black.

Not a single white person was ever arrested or charged in the shootings of any of the black victims of the Elaine Massacre of 1919.

The government of Phillips County did not have the resources to contain 143 prisoners at one time. As a result, it rushed to hold a trial, seeking to punish the guilty and free the innocent. Seventy-three men were indicted under various charges. Most of the men were convicted of lesser crimes and fined or held. Twelve men were accused of first-degree murder. In trials that lasted an average of twenty minutes, the charges were stated, evidence was produced, arguments were heard, and the jury returned a verdict of "guilty." All twelve men were condemned to be executed for the crime of murder.

Outside Phillips County, those who heard the news of the massacre, the arrests, the trial, and the verdict suspected that something was not quite right. The National Association for the Advancement of Colored People (NAACP) decided to hire lawyers and appeal the sentence to a higher court. Scipio Jones was one of the first lawyers hired. At his recommendation, white attorney George W. Murphy was selected to lead the team of lawyers through the appeal process. When Murphy died, Scipio Jones became the de facto leader of the team. Though he did not appear at every hearing of the case—including that which was heard by the U.S. Supreme Court on January 11, 1923—Jones is widely recognized as the attorney who, through a tangled process of appeals and hearings with many legal technicalities, finally won freedom for all twelve defendants. Six were released on June 25, 1923, after the Arkansas Supreme Court noted that their appeal had led to a court order for a retrial, but they had been held without that trial for more than two court terms. The remaining six were given indefinite furloughs by Governor Thomas McRae on January 14, 1925, which granted them freedom but without the benefit of a formal pardon. All the same, the victory was meaningful, not only for the twelve defendants and their attorneys, but for African Americans in Arkansas and in the rest of the United States.

Jones and the other lawyers pointed, of course, to the irregularities in the initial trial—the fact that witnesses had not been cross-examined and that the deliberations of the jury had been unreasonably short. More significantly, Jones pointed to the fact that the defendants were entitled to "a jury of their peers," but the jury pool in this case had been restricted to white residents of Phillips County, even though the defendants (as well as more than half the residents of the county) were black. Although the latter argument was not effective in overturning the verdict in this case, Jones would use the same argument later with positive results.

Some of his colleagues felt that Jones did not go far enough to defend the rights of all African Americans in Arkansas. His work on the Elaine Massacre case was limited to defending his twelve clients, using technicalities of the law to assist them rather than challenging the entire racist system. Even the appearance of Jones in court and in the streets of Little Rock rankled some of his out-of-state colleagues. Stockley reported, "While the NAACP ranted and raved from its safe offices in New York about how Negroes in the South should act, Jones would continue to show up in court immaculately dressed, even something of a dandy with his walking stick that was purely for show. Yes, he had a Cadillac and a chauffeur to drive it. And yes indeed, his wife Lillie had a maid. … Rich white folks had all of those things. Why shouldn't blacks?"

In addition to his involvement in criminal cases, Scipio Jones also worked as a lawyer on many significant cases involving politics in Arkansas. In 1891, early in his career, Jones argued strenuously against the "Separate Coach bill," a state law which separated white and black passengers on public transportation. That measure passed and remained in effect for the rest of his life. Ten years later, Jones, a Republican, was becoming increasingly concerned with efforts of other state Republicans to make the party "lily-white," offering no black candidates and restricting even the right of black citizens to vote. With John A. Robinson and Archie V. Jones, Scipio Jones

*Scipio Africanus Jones was born in Dallas County, Arkansas, during the Civil War.
Educated in Little Rock, he became one of the most successful African American lawyers
in any southern state. Most remembered for his defense of twelve African Americans
arrested after the Elaine Massacre of 1919, Jones was also active in the Republican Party,
fighting to maintain the rights of African Americans to participate in Arkansas politics. In
that endeavor, he was not successful; only after the Civil Rights Act of 1964 did African
Americans gain the rights that had been promised to them at the end of the Civil War.
Jones maintained a moderately wealthy lifestyle, but he also lost considerable money in
several financial investments.* Photo courtesy of the Butler Center for Arkansas
Studies, Central Arkansas Library System.

created the Independent Political League, an effort designed to place African American candidates on the ballot for Pulaski County office. Jones himself ran for the Little Rock school board in an election on May 16, 1903. He drew the opposition of the state's leading newspaper, the *Arkansas Gazette*, which quoted "a prominent Democrat" who said, "The voters must turn out and vote that all possible chance of there being a negro in the school board may be prevented. Of course, he would have no chance ordinarily, but this is an election in which such little interest is taken, because all Democrats are so cocksure of winning that Jones might slip in." On another page, the *Gazette* editorialized, "We believe there will be general agreement that white men can best manage the Little Rock public schools." A turn-out far larger than usual resulted from this coverage—school board elections in Little Rock at that time generally attracted fewer than four hundred voters—and Jones lost the election, drawing only 181 votes of the 2,383 ballots cast.

Jones remained in the Republican Party, though, and continued to fight measures of his party that were meant to discourage black participation. In 1920, party leaders scheduled the state convention at a hotel that did not allow blacks to enter the building. After registering their opposition, Jones and other black Republicans held a separate party convention at the Mosaic Templars' Building on Ninth Street in Little Rock. There they nominated a separate slate of candidates. The national Republican convention recognized the "official slate" and refused to seat those chosen by Jones's group. The point was sufficiently made in Arkansas, though, so the Republican Party promised in 1924 to hold its convention, that year and in the future, in "places where all Republicans can attend." Party officials also promised to expand the party's committee and guarantee two seats to African American members of the party. Scipio Jones was chosen as a delegate from Arkansas to the Republican national convention in 1928 and again in 1940.

In spite of his own party membership, Jones did not limit his lawyerly attacks to the Republicans. In 1930, he and fellow black attorneys sued the Democratic Party of Arkansas, seeking to reverse party rules that prevented black citizens from voting in the party primaries. Jones and his partners lost that suit, as the courts ruled that a political party is a private organization and not subject to the same rules that the government itself must follow. Not until the 1960s did civil rights activists succeed in passing voting rights acts which required the political parties to allow all eligible voters to participate in elections, regardless of their race.

In spite of his work to overcome Jim Crow laws and attitudes in the political system of Arkansas, Scipio Jones still is regarded by some historians as an advocate of the "separate but equal" way of life that was sought by so many Arkansans of European descent. Indeed, Jones agreed with the philosophy of Booker T. Washington, who felt that blacks in the United States should create their own institutions of wealth and social power rather than challenging to enter the structure that had existed before the Civil War. John Bush, founder of the Mosaic Templars of America, also agreed with Washington. The Mosaic Templars sold insurance to African Americans to cover burial costs; they also became a social club like the Masons. Groups like the Templars encouraged black-owned banks and black-owned businesses. Their building on Ninth Street in Little Rock anchored a black-run business district that was both prosperous and lively. It remained so until the changes of the civil rights era, although the construction of Interstate 630 through the neighborhood probably did more than any civil rights changes to terminate the success of the Ninth Street business district.

That neighborhood was invaded in the spring of 1927, when the body of a young white girl was found—molested and murdered—in a church bell tower not far from the area. The prime suspect, a black janitor who worked for that church, was arrested, and white citizens of Little Rock gathered at the jail, threatening to remove and lynch the prisoner. Police Chief Burl C. Rotenberry had anticipated such a gathering and had already removed the suspect to a safe location. During this period of unrest, another African American man, John Carter, was accused of attacking a white woman and her daughter. Some witnesses, it seems, stated that Carter was actually rescuing the woman and her daughter after the horse pulling their buggy began to bolt and escaped their control. The woman's fright at the horse running wild, according to this explanation, was misinterpreted by some bystanders as her fear of being attacked. Though no written sources from 1927 report this account, it is strongly continued by oral traditions.

Carter was seized by a mob before the police could protect him. His lynching prompted a riot of white citizens in the Ninth Street business district that threatened to imitate the Elaine Massacre of recent memory. Scipio Jones, as a leader in the community, was able to spread the word among his fellow African Americans to remain out of sight. Though windows were smashed and stores were looted, and a large bonfire was built in the street, no more lives were lost, and after a few hours the city police were able to disperse the mob.

Precisely that attitude of "stay out of sight and don't fight back" has made some historians question Scipio's attitude toward civil rights. His friends, including John Bush, became wealthy under the "separate but equal" standards of the Jim Crow era. Jones himself was comfortable, but never excessively wealthy. He did have a fancy car, driven by a chauffer, and he did own several houses in Little Rock, but most of his business investments failed to yield the kind of return that Jones obviously would have wanted. Jones was a major stockholder in the Arkansas Realty and Investment Company—intended to help African Americans purchase homes in central Arkansas—and was elected president of the company, but the corporation failed after three years and was dissolved on June 19, 1911. Jones also heavily invested in the People's Ice and Fuel Company of Little Rock, which succeeded at first but ultimately failed at the start of the Depression.

Jones helped the Mosaic Templars purchase $125,000 in Liberty Bonds during the First World War. After the war, he served as director of the United Charities drive, a predecessor of the United Way. He also served on the Board of Trustees for Shorter College, his alma mater. In addition, he volunteered his time to assist the Aged and Orphans Industrial Home in Dexter, Arkansas.

In 1941, Jones persuaded the legislature of the state of Arkansas to provide tuition assistance for African American students from Arkansas who were attending colleges in other states. At that time, Arkansas had only one program of higher education that accepted black students, Arkansas Agricultural, Mechanical, and Normal College in Pine Bluff. (That school has now become the University of Arkansas at Pine Bluff.) The money was provided by the state legislature, which in 1943 appropriated $5,000 for that assistance, but the legislature insisted upon withdrawing the same amount of money from the budget of the college. After World War II, African American students began to be accepted at the University of Arkansas in Fayetteville (in the medical and law departments first, and then in all departments of the school) and ultimately in all the colleges and universities of Arkansas.

Jones was respected by his fellow attorneys in Arkansas. Twice Jones served in a temporary capacity as judge, selected for this honor by his peers, both black and white. He was elected as a special judge to hear a case in the Little Rock Municipal Court when the regular judge disqualified himself. In 1924, Jones again was elected to a special position, serving as a special chancellor in the Pulaski County Chancery Court.

Of course at the beginning of his career, Jones entered into practice in the firms of other lawyers. Before 1917, he shared the offices of several significant African American attorneys of Little Rock, including (at different times) John A. Robinson, Archie V. Jones, John W. Gaines, Thomas J. Price, and Milton Wayman Guy.

From 1917 until his death, Jones retained a solo practice, but in the various trials involving the Elaine Massacre and in many other cases, Jones often worked with other attorneys, some white and some black.

Jones also was not alone in his home life. His first wife, Carrie Edwards Jones, was twenty-five years old when they married on March 14, 1896. Carrie died young, in 1908. They had a daughter, Hazel, who died in Chicago at the age of thirty-five. In 1917, Scipio Jones married Lillie M. Jackson of Pine Bluff. Scipio and Lillie Jones had no children. With Carrie and Hazel, Scipio Jones lived at 1808 Ringo Street in the Dunbar neighborhood of Little Rock. After Carrie died, Scipio and Hazel moved down the block to 1822 Ringo Street. His third house was a Colonial Revival cottage at 1911 Pulaski Street. In 1928, Scipio and Lillie built a house at 1872 Cross Street, a richly detailed Craftsman-style residence. This house is now listed on the National Register of Historic Places.

Scipio Jones died at his home on Cross Street on March 28, 1943. The cause of death listed on his death certificate is arteriosclerosis. His funeral at Bethel AME Church in Little Rock (where he had been a member for over fifty years) was attended by many governmental and political leaders of both races. Notably, the church (which at the time was the largest black congregation in Little Rock) provided a separate section in the building for the seating of the "white friends" of Scipio Jones. He is buried at Haven of Rest Cemetery on West Twelfth Street in Little Rock, an all-black cemetery. Other than the house, the only assets Jones could bequeath to his widow, Lillie, was a bank account which contained a little less than $1,500.

The City of North Little Rock paid honor to Scipio Jones in 1928 by naming its new junior and senior high school for African Americans after the attorney. Either ironically or fittingly, the building was abandoned in 1970 when the North Little Rock school system was desegregated; the building burned down in 1986.

VII

Bernie Babcock:
She Slept in the Basement

B ernie Babcock was not often wrong. Though she was creative and imaginative from an early age, she also displayed the discipline of a historian, only rarely embellishing the truth. Her determination to provide Little Rock with a museum of natural history put her into some awkward situations, such as accepting and defending the contribution of ancient Native American artwork that was almost certainly fraudulent, and feuding with established organizations over space in Little Rock's public buildings. In spite of her few miscalculations, Bernie Babcock could, near the end of her long life, look back favorably on a career of writing and of public service that has helped to keep history alive for thousands of Arkansans and visitors to the state.

Her parents named her Julia Burnelle Smade, but most of her life she wanted to be called Bernie. She was born in Union, Ohio, on April 28, 1868, to Hiram Norton Smade and his wife, Charlotte Elizabeth Burnelle Smade, who went by the nickname Lottie. Bernie was the oldest of six children, and her parents encouraged her free spirit and creativity. According to an interview she gave when she was ninety, Bernie found herself in trouble the very first day she attended a public school. The guest of an older child, she was brought to a kindergarten class in Union when she was three years old. The teacher asked the children in the room to describe an event that had recently happened to them. Bernie reported that, as she was on her way to school that day, "a horse lowered his neck, drew his lip high from his great big horse teeth, and bit my head off." Shocked, the teacher walked Bernie home and accused her of lying. Her mother calmly said, "Oh, that is only a sign that she will be a writer when she grows up." Whether or not Bernie embellished this story to enhance her reputation for embellishing stories, it still reflects the way she was raised, encouraged to see life from her point of view whether or not others approved of her stories. Her grandmother reportedly said that "sinful tendencies came from an abnormal development of her curiosity bump." Bernie later claimed that her "first literary attempt had been made at the tender age of six years, a poem too wonderful for publication being the result."

While she was still a child, her family moved to Russellville, Arkansas. Her father built and operated a sawmill, while her mother became active in the cause of temperance. Women were not yet allowed to vote or to be elected to government positions, but women in America were becoming increasingly politically active, and the prohibition of alcohol was a common cause among educated women across the country. By 1890, over one hundred temperance organizations were active in Arkansas, and a political candidate's position for or against prohibition was a significant factor in success at the polls. One of the largest national organizations seeking to reduce or eliminate the sale and consumption of alcohol was the Woman's Christian Temperance Union (WCTU). Lottie Smade founded the Pope County chapter of the WCTU. When she was fifteen years old, Bernie read an essay to the state's WCTU convention in which she argued against the injustice of requiring expensive liquor licenses for retailers. Rather than reducing the consumption of alcohol, Bernie argued, the sale of liquor licenses gave dignity to the businesses by placing the right to sell whiskey into "the hands of respectable men. This seems to be measuring a man's respectability by his money ... but do you think a drunkard's wife cares where her husband gets drunk?"

Hiram and Lottie were not wealthy, and they could not afford to send their eldest child to college. Undeterred, Bernie applied to a Methodist academy in Little Rock. Called Little Rock University, it had been founded by northern Methodists in 1882. (The Methodist Episcopal Church in the United States had split before the Civil War into northern and southern bodies over the issue of slavery; they would not reunite until 1939. Northern Methodist congregations and schools had closed in Arkansas because of the split, but, following the war, northern Methodists reestablished themselves in Arkansas.) Unable to pay for her tuition or living expenses, Bernie took a job as housekeeper for the family of the president of the university, the Reverend E. S. Lewis. President Lewis, according to Bernie's later recollection, thought that she was "a smart aleck" and tried to make her life difficult with hard and embarrassing tasks. However, Bernie persevered for a year, doing all the work demanded of her, maintaining high grades in her classes, and offering a well-received musical recital at the end of her first year at the university.

In spite of her successful year in college, Bernie chose not to remain in school. She had met William Franklin Babcock, an agent for the Pacific Express Railroad Company, in Little Rock, and in spite of the fact that he was ten years older, the two fell in love and were married on April 1, 1887, in Yell County, Arkansas. The couple moved to Vicksburg, Mississippi, but lived there for only a short time before returning to Little Rock. Will's job required him to travel almost constantly, but he spent as much time at home with his young wife as he could spare. During the eleven years of their marriage, they became the parents of five children: Francis, Charlotte, Lucille, Bill, and Mac. Bernie devoted her spare time to developing a large garden behind their house, and also to creating a library for the family in their home. The first two books in the family library were the Bible and Charles Darwin's *The Origin of Species*.

On March 16, 1898, Will Babcock died following surgery for an intestinal blockage. As a single mother at the end of the nineteenth century, Bernie had fewer choices than single parents have today. Most friends and neighbors expected her to place her five children in the hands of others so she could go to work full-time, or perhaps to marry a second time. She was even offered a job as a school teacher. Instead, Bernie resolved to raise her children and to work in the home so the family would not be separated. Looking at the diary that she had maintained during her husband's illness, Bernie realized that she had potential to be a writer and to support her family through that career. For a year, she wrote manuscripts and mailed them to publishers, only to have each returned with refusal notices. One editor demanded that she acquire a dictionary and learn five new words every day—"how to spell them, how to say them, what their derivation is, and how to use them. And then send me this novel back." Finally, a New York publisher named William P. F. Ferguson decided to give the struggling Arkansas writer a chance.

After a few short stories and poems were published in various periodicals, Bernie Babcock produced a book-length narrative that Ferguson was pleased to publish. *The Daughter of the Republican* was a dramatization of the issues surrounding prohibition, the cause that Bernie had been defending since her high school days. Her publisher compared its success and impact to the abolitionist novel of Harriet Beecher Stowe, *Uncle Tom's Cabin*. Babcock's first book sold 100,000 copies in six months of 1900 and was followed the same year by *The Martyr*, a book with a similar theme. The next year saw the publication of *Justice to the Woman*, a work of fiction which was set in an unnamed state where women were allowed to vote and used their electoral power to defeat a cruel and heartless politician in his campaign for the U.S.

Senate. More novels followed, along with short stories and poems, including the poem "The Man with the Rubber Conscience," which was used effectively in some parts of the United States in the prohibition campaign. The 1902 novel *By Way of the Master Passion* allowed Bernie to display her interest and education in the "fascinating story of evolution" as developed by Darwin and his successors.

Babcock raised her children with the same values of creativity and individuality that had marked her childhood, with the result that her children were identified by neighbors as "the sassiest children" in the area. Bernie insisted, "I tried to teach my children self-respect, and self-respect, it seems to me, includes respect for one's own opinions." When her youngest, Mac, started school, Bernie was able to take a job outside of the home. The *Arkansas Democrat* hired her at $12.50 a week to edit its society page and to write book reviews and editorial pieces. Babcock's newspaper work was unsigned. She continued writing at home at night and, in 1903, she was listed in *Who's Who* for authors and writers, becoming the first Arkansas woman so recognized. Bernie was also the first female telegraph editor in any southern state.

In 1906, Bernie left the *Democrat* to be the editor and publisher of *The Sketch Book*, a quarterly magazine of stories, poems, photography, paintings, drawings, and sheet music. Babcock described *The Sketch Book* as "the most beautiful magazine in the south." All its contributions came from Arkansas residents. In 1908, she published the first anthology ever assembled of Arkansas poetry, which she called *Pictures and Poems of Arkansas.* All this work did not keep her from continuing to create other stories which still promoted her favorite causes of prohibition and women's suffrage.

Babcock's writing took her to Chicago in 1910 and later to New York City for two winters, but she chose to make her home in Arkansas, which she described as a better place to raise her children. Her experiences in those big cities added new dimensions to Bernie's career. In New York she became involved in union causes and in help for the poor. She was particularly interested in what she called "submerged poverty people," a class of low-income workers who would later be labeled by sociologists as "under-employed." At the same time, she began to research psychic phenomena, which would remain among her interests for the rest of her life. She also became more interested in archeology, especially as it related to Native American groups. Back in Arkansas, she became passionately involved in the case of Neal McLaughlin, a resident of the Ozark Mountains who had been imprisoned and sentenced to death. Bernie believed that his conviction had happened because of false accusations and as a result of political corruption. After McLaughlin escaped from prison, Bernie crossed his path during a camping trip and promised to arrange for his pardon. To everyone's surprise— particularly McLaughlin's—Bernie succeeded in her campaign, and Governor Charles Brough personally signed the pardon in front of Bernie and McLaughlin.

As is the case with most successful writers, Babcock gained inspiration for her own work by reading copiously. One article, published in the *Ladies' Home Journal* in November 1908, dramatically shaped Bernie's career. The story described the love affair of Abraham Lincoln and Ann Rutledge, which took place in Salem, Illinois, well before Lincoln rose to national fame, and ended with Ann's death in 1835. The romantic story intrigued Bernie, and she began to research the history behind the romance. In addition to reading the many books already published about Lincoln, Bernie sought people still alive who had known the Illinois lawyer and politician. She went to California to interview Ann's younger sister, and she began a long-running correspondence with the Illinois Historical Association. Her initial book on the love affair, *The Soul of Ann Rutledge*, was published in 1919 and marked Bernie Babcock's greatest literary success. The book remains in print to this day and has been translated into several foreign languages.

Bernie felt an affinity with President Lincoln and ended up writing four more books about his life. She felt drawn to Lincoln's compassion for others and his drive to provide justice for all people. In describing Lincoln, Bernie found a platform to display her own beliefs, saying at the end of *Little Abe Lincoln*, published in 1926, "Greatest of all Americans is he and beloved as no American has ever been for, although the storms of life beat against his soul with a force and cruelty unmeasured, he bore malice toward none and had love for all. Every great artist makes some one work better than all the others. This is called a masterpiece. Among the Great Creator's masterpieces of all the ages is Abraham Lincoln." By the end of the 1920s, Bernie Babcock was widely regarded as one of the world's foremost authorities on the life of Abraham Lincoln.

All the same, Babcock's writing tended more toward historical fiction than toward academic effort. Her books are filled with fictional characters who witness the action while living their own lives. They also contain the private thoughts and conversations of both historical and fictional characters, presenting as fact what could have come only from Bernie's fertile imagination. Bernie was drawn into the lives of great men like Abraham Lincoln so deeply that she seemingly could not help embellishing the historical record by describing what might have been.

Also during the 1920s, Babcock began to be driven by a new passion. She wanted to provide Little Rock and the state of Arkansas with a museum that would display both natural history and human history for public education. Darwin's theory of evolution was being widely challenged in Arkansas and in neighboring states—most famously in the so-called Scopes Monkey Trial, held in Tennessee in 1925. A proposed law that would ban the teaching of evolution in Arkansas public schools was rejected by the General Assembly in 1927, but its supporters were able to circulate petitions placing the law on the ballot for the 1928 election. The initiated act passed, receiving sixty-three percent of the vote, and remained the law of the state until

1968, when a challenge to the law led to its review by the U.S. Supreme Court, which rejected its provisions. While other Arkansans involved themselves in the political process to support or oppose this law, Bernie sought to shape public opinion through education, and she considered a museum of natural history a necessary step to provide such an education to the people of Arkansas.

She was additionally motivated to create this museum by the distain with which outsiders viewed Arkansas, especially people of northern and eastern cities such as Chicago and New York. Perhaps the most notorious critic of the state was famous Baltimore author H. L. Mencken. Writing in 1931 that the people of Arkansas were "too stupid to see what was the matter with them," he drew a roar of protests, including a vote by the General Assembly demanding that Mencken apologize for his characterization of the state. Unfortunately, the resolution calling for an apology misspelled Mencken's name. The rich opportunities for rebuttal were too good for Mencken to refuse, and he continued to write about Arkansas, deliberately continuing and escalating the controversy. After all, Mencken's career as a writer depended upon generating a reaction from his readers, and much of the country was entertained by his disparaging comments and the responses he gathered. Again, Bernie believed that the best answer to opponents like Mencken was not to continue the conversation but to provide evidence of Arkansas's cultural life and intellectual activity. A quality museum, she was convinced, was a necessary ingredient for that cultural life and intellectual activity.

Her first venue for exhibits was a storefront on Main Street. By 1927, she had acquired space on the third floor of Little Rock's City Hall for her expanding collection. It was then necessary to incorporate the museum and place it under control of Little Rock's city government. Naming it the Museum of Natural History and Antiquities, Babcock succeeded in having herself made director of the museum, and she continued seeking additional artifacts and items for display. Some of the items, including a large collection of preserved animals, came from outside of Arkansas. Donors included the Smithsonian Institution in Washington DC and the American Museum of Natural History in New York. A preserved human head, billed as "the head of a Chicago criminal," was also kept on display. Mastodon bones, pearl-bearing mussels from the White and Black rivers of Arkansas, and various "Indian relics" were also featured items in the collection. Bernie acquired many items from around the state of Arkansas, including war memorabilia and pioneer remnants, as well as a great many Native American artifacts.

Babcock's favorite items on display were items carved out of sandstone and decorated with pieces of metal. The items supposedly had been found in the soil of Crowley's Ridge near the city of Jonesboro, Arkansas. The discoverer and marketer of these pieces, Dentler Rowland, however, was a jeweler and gunsmith who was very capable of creating the works of art which he said he had found. The centerpiece of the collection of more than eighty artifacts was a stone bust, twelve to fourteen inches high, depicting a frowning man. The style of the artwork is more similar to the art of the Aztecs of Mexico than to that of any group that ever lived in Arkansas. The eyes of the bust were made of copper and had silver pupils, the ears had gold plugs, and a copper heart was embedded in the neck of the bust. (The heart alone was evidence of fraud, since the familiar heart shape used in American Valentine greetings was not a shape ever used in ancient American artwork.) Other pieces in the collection were later found to contain fragments of metal that came from a twentieth-century horse harness. Bernie was cautious enough to visit the gravel bed where Rowland claimed he had found the sculptures, but her excitement outpaced any reservations she might have felt. Bernie paid $1,000 for the large bust and several smaller pieces, and she exhibited the find in her museum, billing the bust as King Crowley.

She was warned several times over the years that the artwork was a fraud, but Bernie never publicly admitted that she had been mistaken. Experts at the Smithsonian and local historians all studied the work and insisted that it was recently cut sandstone that had been dyed to appear older. They also pointed out that the carvings of a hippopotamus and of a camel certainly could not have been the work of an ancient tribe living in Arkansas. Bernie remained faithful to her heart-felt conviction, and the pieces remained on display.

Meanwhile, the Great Depression was affecting the lives of most people in Arkansas, and Bernie Babcock and her children were not immune to its force. Bernie was generally paid between three hundred and five hundred dollars for a book, one reason that she tried to produce two or three books a year. The museum work was not high-paying either. Bernie had managed to purchase 380 acres of land west of Little Rock. Naming the estate Broadview, she relocated herself there and also provided land for her married children to build homes. Renovating a barn, she continued her delight in gardening while she continued her love of historical research and writing.

For Christmas 1929, Babcock gave the Museum of Natural History and Antiquities to the City of Little Rock as a gift. In 1933, the federal program which was creating jobs for the unemployed, the Works Progress Administration (WPA), needed office space, and the museum was deprived of its third-floor area. Exhibits were crated and put into storage in the City Hall basement. Many items disappeared—newspaper reporters rescued some important museum documents from the City Hall garbage bins. Bernie's anguish at the losses can only be imagined.

The demand of the WPA proved, though, to be a disguised blessing for Bernie. Not all of its projects involved construction and heavy work. Though the WPA is most famous for its building projects—roads, drainage ditches, park cabins, schools, and municipal buildings—it was also providing work for people skilled in other kinds of labor, including writing. The Federal Writers' Project during the

Depression interviewed slaves and their descendants, providing a compelling record of first-person narratives about the last years of slavery in the United States and the lives of former slaves in the years following the Civil War. A smaller series of interviews documented pioneer life in Arkansas and in other states. Still other writers created

Dentler Rowland of Jonesboro discovered artifacts from prehistoric Arkansas buried in Crowley's Ridge in 1923 … or so he claimed. Bernie Babcock believed his claims and purchased many of these artifacts, including a stone carving she named King Crowley. The sandstone in these items matched that on Rowland's farm, and the metal decorations embedded in them (including steel cut from a horse harness) resembled that found in his workshop. The artwork does not match any known North American ancient civilization—one feature on King Crowley is a heart shape familiar today from Valentine's greetings but never used by any ancient civilization. Also, some of the items in the collection represented non-American animals including a camel and a hippopotamus. Photo of King Crowley courtesy of the UALR Photograph Collection/UALR Center for Arkansas History and Culture.

travel guides to the states, highlighting local history along with features worth visiting. In November 1935, Bernie was hired as folklore editor for Arkansas's group of federally funded writers. Before the project was allowed to expire during World War II, Bernie had become the director of the Arkansas Writers' Project. From 1938 until 1940, she also served as president of Arkansas's branch of the League of American Pen Women, an office she had also held in 1920 when the branch was first founded. During this second time at the branch's helm, Babcock helped the group to sponsor the first Arkansas Writers' Conference, which was held at the University of Arkansas in Fayetteville.

The early 1940s brought an end to the New Deal programs along with the American entry into World War II, but for Bernie these years also brought a new opportunity for public service along with pursuit of her own dreams. The City of Little Rock was making changes at its City Park, a thirty-six-acre property on Ninth Street. The land had once belonged to the U.S. government, which in 1840 had completed an arsenal on the property. This arsenal, along with the adjacent St. Johns' College, had figured prominently in the history of Arkansas, especially around the time of the Civil War. After the war, though, it had fallen into decline, and in 1892 the government traded the arsenal and its surrounding property for one thousand acres north of the Arkansas River, where the government built Fort Logan H. Roots. Little Rock had a pond dug on its new property (calling the pond Pittman's Lake) and opened the City Park on Independence Day in 1893. The park hosted a large reunion of Confederate soldiers in 1911, marking the fiftieth anniversary of the beginning of the Civil War. The WPA had renovated the park in a few ways, including construction of the Museum of Fine Arts. Now, Bernie Babcock took an interest in the property.

With the permission of the City of Little Rock, Bernie was able to move the items that remained from the Museum of Natural History and Antiquities out of the City Hall basement and prepare to display them in the arsenal building. Now in her seventies, Bernie made a home for herself in the basement of the building. She was seen every day at work, even climbing ladders to paint murals on the walls. King Crowley was again given a place of honor, as if no doubts had been raised about his authenticity. Visiting other museums and arranging for new material, Bernie was able to acquire Mexican, Assyrian, and Babylonian artifacts. The first item on Bernie's agenda, though, was to identify the building and the park with its most famous son.

In 1880, Captain Arthur MacArthur Jr. was stationed at the arsenal in Little Rock, accompanied by his wife, Mary. She was expecting a child, and family tradition required her to return to the family home in Virginia for the birth. Douglas chose to enter the world ahead of schedule, however, on January 26, leading a Virginia newspaper to report that Douglas MacArthur had been born to Arthur and Mary "while his mother was out of town." Douglas MacArthur would become a national hero, serving as the Supreme Allied Commander in the Southwest Pacific Theater, opposing Japan in the Pacific Ocean and Asia during World War II; and as Supreme Commander of the Allied Powers in Japan following Japan's surrender at the end of the war. In 1950, he was given command of the United Nations forces supporting South Korea at the beginning of that war; however, he was relieved of command after making public statements that conflicted with those of President Harry S. Truman. As the 1952 elections approached, MacArthur was, for a time, regarded as a likely candidate for the presidency of the United States.

The arsenal tower was surrounded by military barracks, and historians are divided in opinion about whether or not the captain's son was born in the tower building itself. Bernie was convinced that he was, and she was able to produce written confirmation of her conviction from Major General William E. Bergen of the U.S. Army. Using this information, Babcock persuaded the City of Little Rock to rename City Park "MacArthur Park," a name it still bears to this day.

These two photos show author Bernie
Babcock early and late in her career.
Babcock had a passionate interest in a
wide range of subjects, including President
Abraham Lincoln, Native American
history and culture, prohibition, women's
suffrage, the rights of the working poor,
and paranormal phenomena. She was
instrumental in having Little Rock's City
Park on Ninth Street renamed for General
Douglas MacArthur, who had been born
there in 1880, and for several years she
owned and maintained the Museum of
Natural History and Antiquities on park
property. Even decades after her death,
many of her books remain in print and are
available electronically. Photo on the
right courtesy of Marcia Camp; photo
below courtesy of the UALR
Photograph Collection/UALR Center
for Arkansas History and Culture.

On March 23, 1952, less than a year after his famous retirement speech to Congress ("Old soldiers never die; they just fade away"), General Douglas MacArthur returned to the city of his birth. In five hours, he visited the park which had been named for him and the church where he had been baptized (Christ Episcopal Church). He also donated several items to the museum, and Bernie dedicated one room of the museum to display his gifts and other mementos of his career.

In 1946, she also moved into the building a statue which had marked the grave of her husband at Oakland Cemetery for many years. Some writers speculate that the statue had been vandalized and required repairs, or that other vandalism at the cemetery had raised worries in Bernie's mind about the safety of the memorial. Bernie had named the statue "Hope," and she now scrubbed it clean and, with the help of eight men, placed it on a base at the top of the staircase. Behind it was a mural painted by Bernie depicting trees and a blue sky scattered with white clouds. A floodlight illuminated the statue.

Bernie may have felt at home in her museum, but she was not welcome to all the guests. One of the oldest women's clubs west of the Mississippi River, the Aesthetic Club of Little Rock, had been holding regular meetings in the arsenal building since 1894. At first, Bernie did not interfere with their continuing schedule of meetings, but in the spring of 1951 she tendered a written request that they surrender their meeting room to the museum to make room for a collection of Egyptian mummies. The ensuing confrontation was battled in the courtroom and in the newspapers, although always with a stiff and polite formality. On the one hand, it was discovered that the Aesthetic Club had no written lease with the city for the use of the building; permission to hold their meetings there had always been based on a spoken agreement. On the other hand, the Aesthetic Club politely reminded the City that the building would have fallen to pieces long ago if it were not for the support of the club. Aesthetic Club members were also important supporters of the museum, but they now began to ask questions about the condition of the museum, chiefly about who owned the items on display—the City of Little Rock and the seven trustees serving on its museum board, or Bernie Babcock, the museum's director. At some point in the two-year discussion, the Egyptian mummies were forgotten and the General MacArthur mementos came to inhabit the room where the Aesthetic Club had been meeting.

Before the negotiations and hearings were concluded (in favor of the Aesthetic Club), Bernie Babcock tendered her resignation to the museum trustees, effective August 31, 1953. Though rumors persisted that her resignation had been forced, Bernie and the trustees all insisted that she was retiring as director because of her age. She was, after all, eighty-five years old in 1953. Bernie presented the museum with a bill for $800, meant to reimburse her for the many items she was "donating" to the permanent collection. With this money, she planned to start a new life for herself.

Over the years, Bernie had sold many pieces of her Broadview estate to fund her other adventures. Now, with the money from the museum, she bought a new piece of land farther west, on Petit Jean Mountain. She bought a small house and had it moved to the site, which overlooked the Arkansas River. She named the new estate Journey's End. Though she evidently had plans to start a writers' colony on the mountain, no other writers joined her there. Instead, Bernie continued writing on her own. In 1959, she published a volume of poetry. *The Marble Woman* was named for the statue she had moved into the museum (although after she left, the second director of the museum had the piece removed). She granted interviews to newspaper reporters, telling one, "I only want to sit on my little mountain and call down the flying saucers!" To another she told the story of her early creativity that had so shocked an Ohio kindergarten teacher.

Bernie Babcock was found dead in her home on Petit Jean Mountain by a neighbor on the morning of June 14, 1962. Though it was early in the morning, she was dressed for the day, sitting in a chair, holding a manuscript in her lap. She was buried at the side of her husband at Oakland Cemetery. The statue "Hope" that had once decorated the grave had been sold, and no one was able to find its new owners. Likewise, King Crowley had disappeared into a private collection, and its current location remains unknown.

Bernie's museum changed its name several times, becoming the Museum of Science and Natural History in 1964, the Arkansas Museum of Science and History in 1983, and the Museum of Discovery in 1998. The same year as its last change of name, the Museum of Discovery moved about a mile north to the Terminal Warehouse Building in the River Market District of Little Rock. In 2001, a new museum, the MacArthur Museum of Arkansas Military History, opened in the arsenal building of MacArthur Park. It includes an exhibit dedicated to Douglas MacArthur and an exhibit dedicated to the Aesthetic Club, but it does not contain any mention of Bernie Babcock.

VIII

John Brown Watson:
"He Knew What He Thought,"
and He Built a College

"If you don't know where you are going," he used to say, "any road will take you there." John Brown Watson was not a man of dreams or visions; he was a man of action. He came to Arkansas in 1928, invited to lead the state's African American school in Pine Bluff, and he transformed it from a struggling vocational institute into one of the most respected institutions of higher learning in the South dedicated to the education of African Americans.

One of his former students wrote of him, "He was a president who could roar at you and throw a disrespectful visitor off the campus bodily, dust off his hands, and walk calmly into the college kitchen, taste the stew and say, 'Aw chef that's good. Fix me a bowl of that' or 'Ah, chef, I wouldn't feed my hogs that stuff. Throw it out.' He could lead his own prayer meetings, teach his own football cheers, sing his own hymn and do his own lectures. He protected his own dignity and protected the respect of his school."

John Brown Watson does not fit neatly into the pattern of what once was called the Southern Negro. He would better be described as a

Texan, in spite of his years in Georgia, Louisiana, and Arkansas. On the campus of Arkansas Agricultural, Mechanical, and Normal College—usually shortened to AM&N—he was known not as Professor Watson or President Watson, but rather Doc Watson. He wore a black cowboy hat and expensive cowboy boots. His overcoat concealed a .45 Colt revolver and a flask of whiskey. Reportedly, he once told a group of students that he had "never even tasted water until I was twenty-one." When the state of Arkansas, struggling through the Great Depression, could not fund new buildings on the campus of the college, Doc Watson found the donors to improve and enrich the campus.

He was born near Tyler, Texas, on December 28, 1869, to Franklin and Crystal Watson. Franklin's father, John Hornage—a plantation owner of Irish descent—had also been the owner of Franklin's enslaved mother. Why Franklin chose to be known by the name "Watson" is a mystery. John Brown Watson's other grandmother, also named Crystal—although the name is recorded with a variety of spellings in different sources—had, according to family lore, stabbed her owner in the belly in Louisiana and escaped to Texas. She was also said to have been descended from a long line of Virginia slaves, extending back to the 1600s. Some people suspect that her husband may have been Cherokee. John's younger brothers have been described as "outlaws," and the entire family seems to have been at home in the rough-and-tumble ways of late nineteenth-century Texas.

John Brown Watson was exceptional, though, in his pursuit of education. When he was seventeen, he passed the county teacher examination and spent the next two years leading a classroom, in spite of the fact that he had never finished school. He then entered Bishop College in Normal, Texas, and spent seven years earning the equivalent of a high school diploma. After teaching for another two years, Watson went east to seek a college education. He began at Colgate University in Hamilton, New York, but transferred the next year to Brown University in Providence, Rhode Island. When asked in later years what brought him to Brown University, Watson answered, "the train." In 1904, Watson was granted a Bachelor of Philosophy degree from Brown and was offered a teaching job at Morehouse College in Atlanta, Georgia. He taught undergraduate classes in mathematics and science. The president of Morehouse, John Hope, was an 1894 graduate of Brown and was the first African American president of Morehouse. Hope and Watson remained friends for the rest of their lives.

While he was living in Atlanta and teaching at Morehouse, Watson became acquainted with the family of Samuel W. Rutherford, especially Samuel's daughter Hattie Louise Rutherford. The Rutherford family was wealthy due to Samuel's position as the head of the National Benefit Life Insurance Company, which he had founded to sell life insurance policies to African Americans who were refused insurance by the white-owned companies in the United States. Hattie was a graduate of Spelman College in Rome, Georgia, and Samuel apparently had plans for her to marry into another wealthy and prosperous family. She had several suitors, and so Samuel tried to dissuade Watson, at one time firmly saying to the teacher, "Watson, you will never claim the hand of my daughter." Watson knew that Hattie's decision was more important than her father's, and so he continued the courtship in person and in writing. In the end, he prevailed, and the two were married on September 25, 1907. The love letters exchanged between Watson and Hattie remain in the hands of the couple's estate; those that Watson wrote exhibit both his warm affection for Hattie and his bold determination that they should be married.

The next year, Watson left Morehouse College. His reasons for leaving have never been clear, but evidence suggests that he had wearied of the frequent meetings and discussions of the faculty at the college which never led to any action. Instead, Watson took a job with the Young Men's Christian Association (YMCA), serving as a secretary of the Colored Men's Department of the International Committee of the YMCA. Following his years with the YMCA,

Watson was given an important position with the Atlanta State Savings Bank, which he then left when he was offered a job as state agent for the Southern Fire Insurance Company. Neither of these brief jobs in the financial world satisfied Watson's desire to be involved in education, but—along with his previous work at the YMCA—they provided Watson with the experience necessary to reenter college life at the administrative level.

This goal was fulfilled in 1923 when Doc Watson was asked to serve as president of Leland College in Baker, Louisiana. Leland College had been established by the American Baptist Home Mission Society to provide higher education to the African Americans of Louisiana. Watson's education at Brown University and his teaching experience at Morehouse College, along with his fifteen years in the business world, made him the perfect fit for Leland College. He brought his Texas-style exuberance into a world that was accustomed to quieter and more straight-laced ways. When he first met his faculty at Leland, they sat quietly, dressed in the style of eastern gentlemen. During the next five years, Doc Watson rebuilt the image they had of themselves and of the school, introducing his own personal spirit of action and adventure.

Doc Watson's success with Leland College caught the attention of people outside of Louisiana. One group that noticed what was happening at Leland was the new board of trustees of Arkansas Agricultural, Mechanical, and Normal School in Pine Bluff, Arkansas. In the more than fifty years that the school had existed, it had already experienced political and personal controversy, as well as institutional changes and even a change of name. Now, the trustees were looking for someone with a proven record who could settle the school into a pattern of success.

The school in Pine Bluff had first begun holding classes in 1875, but its history had roots in earlier action of the U.S. Congress. In 1827, Congress first mandated that each state set aside two townships to establish a public university. Arkansas had dragged its feet in establishing such a university until the Civil War, and a second such requirement from Congress, made in 1862, had of course been entirely ignored by Arkansas, then a part of the Confederate States of America. The new state government, formed in 1864 after Little Rock had been captured by Federal forces, was more willing to obey these acts of Congress, but money was short, and the required university did not come into being until 1872, when Arkansas Industrial University opened its doors in Fayetteville. (This school later became the University of Arkansas.)

Meanwhile, the same state legislature that had funded Arkansas Industrial University also saw the need to create a state institution that would provide higher education for African Americans. The main reason for this decision was the awareness of legislators that freed slaves and their children would have schools built for them, schools that would require teachers, but no qualified African American teachers had been trained in Arkansas. Some teachers had come from northern states at the end of the war, establishing schools of various kinds. Even colleges for African Americans had been opened—Southland College in Helena, founded by Quakers in 1864; Walden Seminary in Little Rock (later Philander Smith College), founded by Methodists in 1877; Arkansas Baptist College, also in Little Rock, founded by Baptists in 1884; and Bethel University in North Little Rock (later Shorter College), founded by the African Methodist Episcopal Church in 1886.

To this collection of church schools was added one state school, Branch Normal College. The word "Branch" signaled that the college was part of the new university in Fayetteville; the word "Normal" meant that the purpose of the college was to train schoolteachers. Nothing in the name signaled that the school was intended for African Americans, but everyone involved in planning and administering the school understood the legislature's intention.

Pine Bluff was chosen because of its location in the Delta region with its concentration of African Americans. Two African American students were accepted as students at Arkansas Industrial University in Fayetteville, but they received private instruction rather than sitting in classrooms with the white students, and neither of them graduated from the university.

Joseph Carter Corbin was the first superintendent of Branch Normal College. He began in 1875 with seven students after serving as Arkansas's superintendent of public education for a two-year term at the end of Reconstruction. One of the few African Americans to be elected to public office during Reconstruction, Corbin saw first-hand the need for a normal college serving African Americans. By 1892 the school was serving 241 students, although that number is somewhat misleading. In order for students to study teaching, it was assumed that they needed students, so the college also included an elementary school and a high school, and those pupils were counted along with the college students actually learning to be teachers. During his years at the helm of the college, Corbin had frequent conflicts with the school's board of trustees and with the state government. He was accused of financial mismanagement and, while no actual wrongdoing on his part was ever proved, he was forced to step down in 1902.

The second superintendent of Branch Normal College was Isaac Fisher. A graduate of the Tuskegee Institute in Alabama, Fisher brought Booker T. Washington's Tuskegee plan to Arkansas. Washington believed in gradual progress for African Americans through non-confrontation. At the college level, he wanted students to learn technical skills as well as academic subjects. Washington was convinced that white Americans would eventually accept African Americans as fellow citizens and equals, but he was also convinced that the best path toward that goal was hard work without any threat of violence or confrontation. Civil rights leaders of his generation and later accused Washington of delaying improvement for African

Americans, but his schools and other programs received considerable support from both white and black Americans.

Fisher redesigned the program at Branch Normal College to emphasize industrial skills such as sewing and machine repair. While he was superintendent, the college granted no bachelor's degrees. Some of Arkansas's politicians were pleased with the change, but members of the school's board of trustees were quite aware that the college was no longer performing its original function of preparing teachers for the classroom. In June 1911 they persuaded Fisher to resign and put two men in charge of the school: Frederick Venegar as principal and William Stephen Harris as his supervisor. Harris, a Pine Bluff businessman, quickly generated a great deal of opposition from the student body, not because he was white, but because of his inappropriate behavior and patronizing attitude toward the students. An unwelcome gift of black stockings to one female student in 1915 finally provoked a general strike and protest among the students, leading to the dismissal of Harris and Venegar. During the next fourteen years, three different men—Jefferson Ish Jr., Charles Smith, and Robert Malone—served as principal of the school, but none of them were granted sufficient power by the trustees to exercise real leadership in the development of the school.

Changes were happening, though, as the state government became more involved in steering the school. Act 568 of 1921 changed the name of the institution from Branch Normal College to Arkansas Agricultural, Mechanical, and Normal School, beginning a process of separating the institution from the University of Arkansas in Fayetteville, a process that was completed by two acts passed by the General Assembly in 1927. The elementary and high school continued to be counted as part of the larger student body, but two years of instruction were provided at a college level, making AM&N a junior college. New property was acquired for the school, two miles from downtown Pine Bluff and one mile from the existing campus. The thirty-five acres of the new campus were located on U.S. Highway 79 and were close to the Cotton Belt Railway tracks, making the school more accessible to students. Eight buildings were initially planned for the campus, and a one-hundred-acre farm was acquired to help develop the agricultural department of the school. In 1910 the State of Arkansas had created four new colleges with such an emphasis, but all four schools accepted only white students. Now, AM&N was beginning to rise to its potential as a true land-grant college.

The new members of the AM&N Board of Trustees wanted new leadership for the school. They had heard of John Brown Watson at Leland College, so in April 1928 they sent a committee of seven representatives to Louisiana to interview Doc Watson and ultimately invited him to take charge of AM&N. Hearing their proposal and their plans for the school, Watson agreed. On June 1 he was elected as the first president of the fifty-three-year-old institution. Though his formal inauguration was not held until April 14, 1930 (timed to coincide with the dedication of the new campus and buildings), Doc Watson immediately took charge of the institution. One of his first changes happened so quietly that few people noticed at the time, and most researchers since that time have assumed that it already had happened. With an eraser, Doc Watson changed the name of the institution from Arkansas Agricultural, Mechanical, and Normal School (the name given by official legislation in 1921 and affirmed by the General Assembly in 1927) to Arkansas Agricultural, Mechanical, and Normal College. With that one-word change, which was reflected in all school publications and correspondence from that moment on, Watson signaled to the state and to the world his intention to lead a proper institution of higher education and not merely a technical institution of the Tuskegee model.

As Doc Watson later wrote in his unpublished autobiography, "My Life," he had two immediate goals for the college: "to restore the confidence with respect of the colored people" and to win also the interest and respect of white citizens, especially those in government. "I found the college a prey of cheap politics and without the respect of the people of the state—white and Negro people," he wrote, adding, "Nothing could be gained by indirect and compromising method. The situation demanded patient and sincere effort on the part of the president and faculty." Estimating that 350 African American students from Arkansas had enrolled in out-of-state colleges because of their lack of respect for AM&N, Watson was determined from the start to make the college an attractive choice—in fact, he wanted the school to be the obvious choice for Arkansas students choosing a college.

Doc Watson immediately arranged for the school to be a four-year college rather than merely a junior college. At the same time, he arranged for night classes to continue vocational instruction for African Americans beyond the typical college age—today described by colleges as "non-traditional students." He introduced an athletic program to the school, arranging a football schedule that included Shorter College, Philander Smith College, and Arkansas Baptist College, as well as similar schools in Oklahoma, Tennessee, and Texas. Track and basketball—both men's and women's teams—were also added to the school. A debate club was formed in the spring of his first year. Watson also demanded that each college student have a physical examination and arranged for doctors and dentists from Pine Bluff to visit the campus and conduct these exams at no cost to the students. He required daily devotions, Sunday school and Sunday evening services, and a weekly prayer meeting on Wednesday nights. He arranged for concerts, plays, and other cultural events to take place on campus. He discouraged dancing and forbade alcohol and tobacco. He also refused to allow fraternities and sororities, saying that such societies were too expensive for college students.

Some faculty left during the first year or two of Watson's administration. Watson clearly encouraged at least some of them to leave. Many new instructors were added to the faculty. More and more each year, the body of teachers resembled the personality of Doc Watson. One young man, Silas Parker, walked to Pine Bluff because he had heard about the college and what it had to offer. He met Doc Watson on campus and asked how he could take classes without money to pay for tuition or room and board. "Do you know anything about horticulture?" the president of the college asked. "Yes, sir," Parker stammered, even though he had never before heard the word "horticulture" and had no idea what it meant. "You can sleep on the floor of the gym," Watson offered, "and eat one sweet potato a day from the farm. The rest of your bills will be paid." Parker worked on the college's farm, took classes, earned his degree, and eventually earned a doctorate in horticulture. He joined the faculty of AM&N and oversaw the college farm; every week, two bushels of fresh vegetables were delivered to the president's house on campus.

Doc Watson was not content to focus on the training of teachers (the original purpose of the school) or on vocational training for African Americans (as the school had been adapted to provide). He was determined to offer a full college education, including the sciences and the liberal arts. He was also determined that AM&N become a fully accredited college, recognized not only by organizations of African American schools, but by the regional organizations that oversee all colleges and universities. To this end, he pushed the members of the faculty to earn higher degrees in their areas of expertise. AM&N was accredited by the State Board of Education of Arkansas in 1932, and also received accreditation from the Southern Association of Colleges and Secondary Schools that year. Doc Watson wanted accreditation as well from the North Central Association of Colleges and Secondary Schools. North Central withheld accreditation, though, both on the grounds of a lack of academic accomplishments by the school's instructors and because the organization felt that salaries were too low at AM&N. The accreditation Watson sought was finally earned, but not until 1950.

The new campus was completed and in use by the end of 1929. It featured eight buildings, including men's and women's dormitories, an administration building, a home economics building, an arts and science hall, a training building for teachers, a power plant, and the president's home. This construction is particularly impressive given the fact that Arkansas was already suffering significant economic difficulties. Agriculturally based states like Arkansas did not require a stock market crash to signal a depression; the Great Depression was already effectively under way in Arkansas by 1929. Low prices for cotton and other farm products, combined with devastating natural

Many governmental leaders in Arkansas in the early twentieth century believed that college education for African Americans should train them only for menial jobs such as sewing and machinery repair. Graduate courses in medicine and law at the University of Arkansas, Fayetteville, were not open to African American students until after World War II. President Watson at Arkansas AM&N in Pine Bluff ensured that science and the liberal arts were taught to students as well as vocational skills. Paradoxically, he opposed the creation of graduate programs at AM&N, both out of fear that accreditation for the programs might be withheld and out of hope that graduates of AM&N would be accepted into graduate programs at the state's other schools. Photo courtesy of the John Brown Watson Estate and of the John Hay Library Special Collections at Brown University.

disasters such as the Flood of 1927 and the Drought of 1930–1931, meant less money for the average citizen of Arkansas and less tax income for the government of Arkansas. Politicians continued to promise new government projects such as better roads and better schools, but often the economic reality was too harsh to allow such political promises to be kept.

AM&N was an exception to this pattern. Fifteen additional buildings were erected on the campus by 1940. Many of these were constructed by federal New Deal programs such as the Works Progress Administration (WPA). Even federal programs required matching or contributing funding, though, and when the powers of Arkansas were unable or unwilling to find money for AM&N, Doc Watson proved able to raise money for the school on his own. Watson's family in Texas sent some money to Arkansas, and other contacts Watson had made earlier in his career also helped him with funding or with connections to new sources of funding. When additional farmland adjacent to the college's farm became available during the Depression, Watson first rented the land for five years and then purchased it himself in 1937 for $1,000. The college continued to use the land for another three years at no cost to the school. Reportedly, enough food was raised on the college's model farm to feed all the students and faculty on campus.

In addition to building programs, AM&N participated in several other New Deal efforts to overcome the Great Depression. The campus was home to Camp Bethune, a National Youth Administration (NYA) program where unemployed and unmarried black women between the ages of eighteen and twenty-five could receive vocational training while also taking classes in English, social studies, and other academic subjects. Students lived in tents on campus and ate in the school cafeteria; they had physical education classes and various social opportunities including their own student government and a camp newspaper. Two sessions of the camp were held, in 1937 and 1938, before government support disappeared. A total of 110 women attended and benefited from camp opportunities.

Not only did Doc Watson support the NYA camp—his wife was made director of the camp. Throughout their years at Leland College and at AM&N, Hattie was as much a part of the schools as her husband. She helped him to create the college catalogue and school newspaper at AM&N, both called *The Arkansayer*. She also began work at the school library, remaining in that position even after Doc Watson died. Hattie never gave birth to a child, but she and Doc Watson adopted a daughter whom they named Marian Anderson Watson, honoring the famed African American singer Marian Anderson. Marian Watson grew up on the campus of AM&N and later attended the Juilliard School in New York before enjoying a successful television career in New York. Since her mother's death in 1974, Marian has continued to maintain the family home in Pine Bluff.

Doc Watson's direct approach was not always appreciated or admired. One researcher points out that more than fifty teachers left the college between 1928 and 1941, quoting Watson's statement, "The College has too little money to keep teachers who are not at least [of] average value to the College," but also saying that Watson "was accused of firing a teacher at the drop of a hat." In 1941, as part of his report to the trustees, Watson wrote, "I have not required the faculty to agree with me in everything and some of them have felt free from time to time to differ with me in some minor matters. Always a few have preferred to air their differences to others. In a few fundamentals, however, I have not allowed anyone to turn me away from some guiding principles I have tried to follow as a school teacher." His natural tendency was to hire teachers who approached education and life with his own style: respectful to others but not timid, men and women of action rather than those who preferred to sit together and discuss a problem instead of working to end a problem.

On one occasion, though, Doc Watson learned that one of the teachers was working with some of the college's trustees to try to have him dismissed as president. Watson assembled the entire faculty and demanded to know which of them was the "turncoat." No one

John Brown Watson treasured education at all stages of life. As president of Arkansas Agricultural, Mechanical, and Normal College (now the University of Arkansas at Pine Bluff), Doc Watson emphasized not only vocational skills but also a full range of college experiences. He brought athletic competitions and performances of the fine arts to the campus. However, he disapproved of fraternities and sororities because he thought that such activities were a waste of the students' hard-earned dollars. This candid snapshot shows him reading a book to his daughter, Marian. Photo courtesy of the John Brown Watson Estate and of the John Hay Library Special Collections at Brown University.

volunteered the information. A second and a third time he asked, and still no one confessed. "Then you all are fired," he roared, and left the room. Later that day, some of the faculty privately told Doc Watson the name of the "turncoat," and in the end most of them were allowed to keep their jobs.

Described as a "firm if not strict disciplinarian," Doc Watson rarely faced direct opposition from any student at AM&N. One exception took place in the spring of 1936 when, for reasons no longer remembered, Watson called one student a "dirty little skunk and a liar." According to the *Chicago Defender*, students rose to her defense in a campus riot that was "marked by the brandishing of guns, throwing of bricks, and the expulsion of three members of the class, one of them its president." Watson met with the senior class and promised a public apology to the student. At first the incident appeared to be over, but Doc Watson then dissolved the student council and threatened not to confer degrees on the graduating class unless they all attended a previously scheduled reception at his home. The seniors did attend the reception, but while it was being held, rocks were thrown through the window of the house and electric power was turned off all over the campus. Though no arrests were made, some of the people involved were "rounded up at gun point and 'hustled off the campus.'" That month, twenty-three students did receive their bachelor's degrees, six received junior college degrees, and twenty-three received high school diplomas.

Not all of Watson's opposition came from within the college. Many white Arkansans resented Doc Watson's success in providing a college education, rather than simply vocational training, to Arkansas's African Americans. One evening, Doc Watson summoned several members of the faculty to his home on campus. Each was handed a shoebox but was told not to open the box until all those invited had arrived. When they were all assembled, Doc Watson told the teachers that he had learned that some of the white citizens of Pine Bluff were planning to invade the campus and attack the power plant. The teachers would be Doc Watson's guards to defend school property. Told next to open their boxes, each man found himself provided with a loaded handgun. One of them protested that he did not know how to fire a gun. "You just aim the gun and pull the trigger," Doc Watson answered. No record of an armed conflict between white townspeople and the school faculty has been found. Very likely Doc Watson made it known that the teachers were armed and prepared to protect the school, and this news alone was sufficient to prevent the attack.

Doc Watson also had to do battle with the state legislature to ensure that the college continued to receive the funding to which it was entitled. On one occasion he is said to have told several legislators, while pointing first to his fist and then to his head and finally to his mouth, "I will fight you with this … and I will fight you with this … and I will fight you with this!" Another time he received word that an important debate was happening in Little Rock involving the school and his voice might be needed at the capitol. Doc Watson had two chauffeurs, but at the moment neither was available. Jumping into his car, he sped up the gravel road to Little Rock, until he reached a ninety-degree bend in the road. The car, of course, left the road. Whether Doc Watson reached Little Rock that day and whether the college benefited or lost from the debate is not remembered. The incident was remembered on campus, though, and that bend in the road was long after called "Watson's Curve."

Perhaps the oddest opposition Doc Watson faced was from fellow African Americans and other civil rights advocates who misunderstood what he was trying to do. Watson fought to keep AM&N a true college and to give a complete education to its students. He resisted any effort by the state government or by others to limit its instruction to vocational training. Yet he is a misunderstood figure in African American history. Many writers, when they mention Watson at all, speak of him as an advocate of Booker T. Washington's

Tuskegee program. Watson was good friends with W. E. B. Du Bois; but Du Bois's principal biographer, David Levering Lewis, scarcely mentions Watson at all in his writing. When he does, he describes Watson as a "Bookerite" and quotes Watson's words out of context to suggest that he wanted to preserve the racial segregation of the Jim Crow era and encouraged African Americans not to resist segregation.

Doc Watson did tell students that it was better for them to remain on southern farms than to relocate to northern cities looking for work. His reasons for that statement were, first, that Watson knew that racism and segregation existed in the northern cities every bit as much as in the South; and, second, Watson knew that conditions for African Americans in the South would never improve if their best and brightest left with the hope of better promises elsewhere.

In 1931, Doc Watson published an essay in the *Arkansas Democrat* in which he advocated increased support for colleges like AM&N. "One very essential thing is to remove from the minds of white people the idea that the negro is ambitious for political and social control," he wrote. "The fact is that as the negro becomes educated he finds increasing satisfaction among the members of his own race. If white people would pop unexpectedly into negro homes they would be surprised at the conditions there, and would then understand why the negro finds satisfaction in his own circle." Doc Watson was not arguing on behalf of continued segregation. Few things would have pleased him more than to have white families visiting black families and becoming better acquainted. Instead, Doc Watson was confronting one of the common excuses given for denying college education to African Americans. Seeking equal education and equal opportunity was not seeking "political and social control," according to Watson. Those who, at the time, held such control had nothing to fear from permitting the African Americans among them to have all the benefits of education that they wanted for their own children and grandchildren.

Given Watson's effort to make AM&N a first-rate college, some members of Arkansas's state government suggested that the college begin offering graduate classes as well as undergraduate degrees. Doc Watson resisted their suggestion. He knew that the faculty was not yet equipped to teach classes at the graduate level; in fact, he was still fighting for accreditation of the school at the undergraduate level. Moreover, he secretly hoped that African American students would be able to take their bachelor's degrees from AM&N and be accepted into graduate programs at the University of Arkansas and other schools in the state which offered graduate classes. His efforts to promote that idea backfired, though. When Watson, with the support of attorney Scipio Jones, pointed out to the General Assembly that African American students had to leave the state to take graduate courses and suggested that the State of Arkansas provide funding to cover some of their educational expenses, the General Assembly agreed. In 1943 they set aside $5,000 to fund those educational expenses, and immediately reduced the state's funding of AM&N by exactly that amount.

During his early years at AM&N, Doc Watson was twice accused of financial improprieties. No doubt knowing that such accusations had plagued Isaac Fisher before him, Watson demanded a full financial review by the trustees of the school and was exonerated. In 1941 a committee led by William Harold Flowers—a Pine Bluff attorney who would become a civil rights leader in Arkansas—asked Governor Homer Adkins to decentralize AM&N. Flowers and his committee were among those who wanted the college to add graduate courses, but at the time Doc Watson was able to prevail on this issue.

The Watson family made many friends in Pine Bluff, including the Bratton family. Wiley Bratton later became a civil rights leader in Arkansas and was one of the students who was accepted into graduate studies at the University of Arkansas in Fayetteville after World War II. When Wiley's brother Leo got into trouble in

Pine Bluff for trying on a suit at a men's clothing store which the store owner had wanted to sell to a white customer, Leo was advised by the local police to leave town. Doc Watson told the faculty and students about the incident and informed them that he would fire or expel anyone who patronized that store.

On December 7, 1942, Arkansas newspapers were filled with war news and reminders of the first anniversary of the attack on Pearl Harbor. They also carried, in small items, the sad news that President John Brown Watson of Arkansas Agricultural, Mechanical, and Normal College in Pine Bluff had died of a heart attack the night before. A memorial service was held in the college chapel, but he was buried in Atlanta, Georgia, after services were held at Morehouse College. Arkansas Agricultural, Mechanical, and Normal College was merged into the University of Arkansas system in 1972, over the protests of many alumni and faculty; it is now known as the University of Arkansas at Pine Bluff (UAPB). Today the school describes itself as a "historically black college" that has a "diverse student population." Several school presidents and boards tried to introduce graduate courses to the curriculum at UAPB, although for years they were met with opposition from the administrators of the University of Arkansas system. Finally, in 1990, graduate courses were added to the university.

One of the histories of AM&N gives this description of President John Brown Watson: "He stood tall; he looked straight; he knew what he thought; he minced no words; he fought with words, deeds, and hands for the building of this college." Many lives were shaped for the better by this Texan who spent the last years of his life developing an Arkansas college. The campus library at UAPB proudly bears his name and displays his portrait.

As for Watson's favorite saying, famous author Lewis Carroll wrote of a conversation Alice had in Wonderland with the Cheshire Cat. Alice asked,

"Would you tell me, please, which way I ought to walk from here?"

"That depends a good deal on where you want to get to," said the Cat.

"I don't much care where," said Alice.

"Then it doesn't matter which way you walk," said the Cat.

A literary man like Doc Watson surely knew about this story, and perhaps he had it in mind when he said, "If you don't know where you are going, any road will take you there." All the same, Watson was far more interested in *doing* rather than merely planning or dreaming. He was well prepared to follow any road, just to see where it might take him, and he invited others to walk the same way.

IX.

Connie Franklin:
After He Was Murdered,
He Came to the Trial

What happens when a murder trial is interrupted by the unexpected appearance of the victim, called to testify on behalf of the defendants? Such an event might be considered too improbable to be used in the script of a movie or television show, yet it happened in December 1929 in Mountain View, the county seat of Stone County in northern Arkansas. Even before Connie Franklin appeared in town to prove that he had not been murdered, the case was receiving international attention for its many bizarre and improbable elements. The story did not end with Connie's surprise revelation, though, because the chief witness for the prosecution, Connie's fiancée, emphatically and repeatedly denied his identity, saying, "That's not my Connie!"

Outside of Stone County, the strange case of Connie Franklin remained largely forgotten for eighty years. Early in the twenty-first century, however, historian Brooks Blevins took an interest in the case, researching its details and speaking and writing about the alleged murder and the subsequent trial. Shortly thereafter, the descendants of the accused murderers began using public media such as Wikipedia to publish accounts of the events, accounts which fully exonerated the accused murderers. Blevins took less interest in solving the "cold case" than in examining what it said about the public image of the state of Arkansas. He noted how the preconceived notions of reporters from Kansas City and other more remote cities flavored their description of the case, deepening the same prejudices of their readers. He also noted how Arkansans, particularly Governor Harvey Parnell and the editors of the *Arkansas Gazette* and *Arkansas Democrat*, decried the false image created by those reporters. The image of Ozark hillbilly life would continue to be displayed throughout the twentieth century by cartoons such as *L'il Abner*, radio shows like *Lum and Abner*, the comedy of Bob Burns, and movies such as *Bloody Mama* and *The Legend of Boggy Creek*.

The image created by newspaper reporters of life in Stone County might easily have inspired any number of low-budget movies or television shows. Consider this scenario: a small number of wealthy and powerful families control the entire political and economic life of a region, including law enforcement and the courtroom. The rest of the citizens, closed off from the world, are too intimidated to challenge the system—anyone who does show the smallest sign of opposition is rapidly punished and quieted. Newspaper reports in 1929 used words such as "barons," "peonage," and even "slavery" to depict conditions in Stone County. They suggested that the working population was deliberately deprived of education and of religion to keep them in line. Blevins has demonstrated that the citizens of Stone County were neither illiterate nor churchless, but he does acknowledge a socioeconomic division that may have contributed to the alleged murder and its aftermath. Moreover, in his research he has demonstrated the existence in Stone County of a sort of "vigilante justice" generally associated with the Ku Klux Klan and other organizations of its ilk. While the outlandish prose of the reporters describing peonage and land barons needlessly exaggerated conditions of the Ozark region, life was harder in the Ozarks than in most places, because in Arkansas the Great Depression had begun years before the stock market crash of 1929. Bad weather and low prices, combined with malnutrition and rampant disease, made it difficult for the typical Ozark farmer to escape poverty. As a result, though the Ozarks did not have plantations like those of the Delta region in Arkansas, the area still preserved a separation between the moderately wealthy elite and the struggling majority of the population.

Into this world drifted Connie Franklin, a wanderer who gave no clues about his past and was known more for his musical abilities than for his work ethic. He appeared in the tiny town of St. James in January 1929, earning enough to support himself by cutting railroad ties and firewood, and entertaining those who would listen by singing ballads and playing the harmonica. One of those who would listen was Tiller Ruminer. (In various records her first name is given as Tilla or Tillar rather than Tiller.) She was the oldest child of Charley and Luella Ruminer, who (according to census records) were also the parents of George, Hoyt, Lloyd, Floyd, Vica, and D. H. Ruminer, although Lloyd apparently died before 1930. Sixteen years old when she met Connie Franklin, Tiller was, according to all accounts, swept off her feet. Connie evidently was taken by the young girl as well—and in 1929, sixteen was not too young an age for the romantic interests of a man in his twenties. On March 9, 1929, Connie and Tiller walked to the house of Finis Ford, the justice of the peace, planning to ask him to marry them. Ford was not at home, and the two left on foot, making plans for the next visit and the wedding to follow shortly.

Connie Franklin was not seen in St. James, or anywhere in Stone County, after that night, at least not until December when the murder trial was about to begin. At first Tiller Ruminer was close-mouthed about the disappearance of her boyfriend. His knapsack, containing his few possessions, was left behind in the room where he had been staying. Mail addressed to Connie continued to arrive at the St. James post office. People were talking, but no one who knew what had happened to Connie was saying anything. Among the people who were talking was Bertha Burns, who had a reputation as the community gossip but who also is reported to have heard "anguished cries" during the night of Connie's disappearance.

Bertha also had one piece of evidence: a blood-soaked hat that appeared to be Connie's. On the basis of the community gossip and the hat, county sheriff Sam Johnson conducted an investigation and called a grand jury to assemble in May, but the grand jury took no action, largely because there was no eyewitness to describe what had happened to Connie. A woman who said she was Connie's sister visited St. James that summer, but evidently no one was able to tell her anything about the drifter either.

Things changed that fall. Sam sat down with Tiller, promising her that no harm would come to her if she told him the truth about Connie and about what had happened that night. The story she then related both shocked and appalled the sheriff. Tiller said that, as she and Connie returned from their fruitless journey on March 9, they were waylaid by four men in a remote part of the county. These men attacked Connie and beat him to unconsciousness. Two of them then dragged Tiller into the woods and raped her, while the other two carried the unconscious body of Connie to a bonfire and threw him into the fire. According to Tiller, when the body rolled out of the fire, the men laughed, dismembered the body, and threw the pieces back into the fire. "Tortured, mutilated, and killed" was the summary of what had supposedly been done to Connie Franklin.

Some reports of Tiller's account claim that she then said she was held against her will by the four men for a period of two weeks, during which she continued to be sexually assaulted. Other evidence indicates that she was home with her parents by the next evening, and she never testified under oath that she had been imprisoned. The one instance of violence against Tiller and her fiancé was horrifying enough, but adding to the surprise, Tiller provided the names of the attackers. They were not strangers to the community, nor were they considered the lowest class of society. Instead, they were the sons of the wealthier families (wealthy being a relative term in this part of the country and at this time in American history). The men Tiller accused of raping her were Hubert Hester and Herman Greenway; the other two, those who mutilated and burned Connie's body, were Joe White and Bill "Straight-Eye" Younger. All four came from respected families of the area. Their reputation was not that of violent criminals, but rather of Ozark enforcers, the self-appointed defenders of the law who were opponents of moonshiners and other undesirable elements.

This sort of extra-legal vigilante justice was common all over Arkansas in the first half of the twentieth century, not just in the Ozark hills. In addition to the Ku Klux Klan, similar groups were identified as bald knobbers, night riders, and whitecappers. All of them dedicated their energy to preserving their version of law and order. African Americans were frequently victims of their attacks, sometimes to the point of lynching and race riots. (Stone County, however, had only fifteen African American residents in 1929.) Other "undesirable" members of the population who could expect trouble from such groups included Roman Catholics, organizers of labor unions, and men accused of drunkenness or infidelity. In some parts of Arkansas, night riders used violence and the threat of violence to try to control prices paid for harvested cotton. In mining communities and railroad towns, the threat of violence from such groups was directed at immigrant populations who might be suspected of any kind of aberrant behavior ranging from public drinking to labor agitation.

Assuming for the moment that Tiller's accusations were true (and it must be remembered that none of the four men were ever convicted of any criminal behavior taking place on that night), what would motivate such a violent and vicious attack upon the young couple? The only apparent reason for the attack is that Connie, an outsider, had won the heart of one of the local girls. If the brutal attack did indeed take place as Tiller described, the men might have seen their actions as suitable retribution for an undesirable romance, as well as a warning to be heeded by other drifters that Stone County girls were off-limits to them. This explanation fits the reporting of the out-of-town newspapers that described the landowners of the county as barons who demanded full control over the lives of those who served them.

On the other hand, if Tiller was lying about the attack, what motive might have prompted such a lie? Researchers attempting to answer that question have focused their suspicion not on Tiller alone, but also on Bertha Burns. She and her husband had been subject to a beating at the hands of the local vigilantes, and she may have wanted revenge upon those involved, as well as an opportunity to challenge the prevailing system of the community. In fact, during the trial in December, it was suggested by the prosecution that the accusations of rape, torture, and murder were the latest stage in a feud that had been simmering for eight years. Would Bertha's itch for revenge give her sufficient leverage to persuade Tiller to create and maintain such a horrifying lie? It happens that Tiller and her family were victims of a similar attack on March 10, the day after Connie was last seen in St. James. Her father, Charley, was beaten in his home by four men, one of whom accused Charley of stealing from him; according to later testimony, they threatened Tiller and her mother but did not strike them, and they held Hoyt Ruminer for a time as hostage "to make sure you [Tiller] don't squawk." Whatever other explanations might be found for the mysterious disappearance of Connie Franklin, this event might have given Tiller sufficient cause to testify against her neighbors.

Whether the men were innocent or guilty, more evidence was needed even to hold a trial than merely a blood-stained hat and the word of Tiller Ruminer. Bertha Burns conveniently located the missing evidence. In the autumn of 1929, just ten days before the grand jury was to convene to consider whether or not a murder trial was to be scheduled, Bertha led the sheriff to a pile of ashes in the woods that was old enough to have been a bonfire back in the springtime. In those ashes were found some scarred pieces of bone—whether animal bone or human bone could not be quickly determined. Sheriff Johnson sent the bones to the state's crime lab in Little Rock, and the grand jury set a date of December 16 for the trial. Sheriff Johnson arrested five men: Hester, Greenway, White, Younger, and also Alex Fulks, identified by Bertha Burns and others as the ringleader of the gang that had so terrorized Stone County over the past years.

Following the grand jury decision and the arrests, interest in the crime grew across the country. Reporters from Kansas City began sharing the lurid details of the charges, and soon newspapers in New York, Chicago, and other major cities were carrying the story. Wire services sent reports around the world. Weekly magazines such as *Time* devoted space to the coming trial. Nearby newspapers, including the *Arkansas Democrat*, the *Arkansas Gazette*, and the *Memphis Commercial Appeal* carried daily coverage of the upcoming trial. To prevent an escape, and to provide greater security for the accused, Sheriff Johnson separated the five men and sent them to three neighboring counties: Greenway and White to Batesville in Independence County, Hester and Younger to Newport in Jackson County, and Fulks—the alleged ringleader—to Melbourne in Izard County. Hugh Williamson, the prosecuting attorney, and his brother Ben Williamson, the defense attorney, carefully prepared their cases, working out of the same law firm in Mountain View. The five accused men insisted that they had not seen Connie Franklin on the night when he disappeared. Hugh built his case around the physical evidence—Connie's hat and the bones found in the pile of ashes— and around the testimony of Tiller Ruminer and of one other man,

Reuben Harrell. Harrell was twenty years old, was a cousin of Tiller, and could neither hear nor speak. His written testimony, though, said that he had been in the woods the night of the crime and had seen a man carrying Connie's body.

The state examiner, J. W. Garrison, was prepared to testify that one of the bones found by Bertha Burns and Sheriff Sam Johnson was, in fact, a remnant of a human skull. Following that examination, the bones were stored in an old coffee can kept in the sheriff's office. Alex Fulks, accused of being the gang's ringleader but never mentioned in Tiller's or Reuben's testimony, succeeded in having his case separated from the main case to be heard on its own merits. The case being reported in the media already seemed determined against the defendants, but rumors began to be heard that Connie Franklin might not be dead after all. Putting their hope in these rumors, family members of some of the defendants offered a reward to anyone who could produce the living Connie Franklin before the trial began.

On December 5, newspapers began to report the unexpected news that Connie Franklin had indeed been found. The earliest report to be printed stated that on March 15, 1929, Connie had stumbled onto the farm of Elmer Wingo of the Morrilton area, his clothing torn and charred in places and his body and face bruised. (Wingo also told reporters that Connie had worked for him earlier and had celebrated his twenty-first birthday with the Wingo family in 1927.) According to Wingo, Connie said that he had been beaten by a gang of men who ordered him to leave the community, then forced him to drink liquor until he passed out and slept through the night. After his recovery at Wingo's farm, Connie apparently continued to drift around the state, working at odd jobs but generally staying out of the public eye. He worked the cotton fields in Adkins bottoms and then headed for the rice country in Arkansas County. He of course had no idea of the accusations that had followed his disappearance from St. James, but reporters and law enforcement officers, as well as concerned citizens—

both those interested in the truth and those interested in the reward money—all were excited to know that Connie was alive and well. On December 7, he was located at a farm near Humphrey, between Little Rock and Pine Bluff. Cotton buyer F. K. Marks took credit for the discovery, as Connie was whisked up to Batesville in a high speed chase involving several reporters all vying for the valuable scoop in this most interesting story.

At Batesville, Connie visited Greenway and White at the county jail. Before any word had been said to them about their visitor, they recognized him and greeted him by name. The reunion was joyful on both sides, and those present were convinced that the man who had been brought to town was the real Connie Franklin. After his stop in Batesville, he proceeded to Stone County. There, at the county seat in Mountain View and in the little town of St. James, Connie was reunited with others who had known him during his several-weeks' stay at the beginning of the year. Many people recognized him, but some doubted. Among the doubters was his fiancée, Tiller Ruminer. Bursting into tears, she wept, "That's not my Connie." The doubted visitor tried to win her over with kind words and caresses, as well as singing for her the same love songs that had won her heart months earlier. Tiller remained adamant that the man who had returned to Stone County was not the Connie Franklin who had won her heart. Others concurred with her opinion, convinced that the Connie they remembered from the first part of the year was considerably younger than the Connie who had arrived in the last month of the year. Tiller told reporters at first that the man who claimed to be Connie "may be Connie Franklin, but he has changed since I saw him last." Later, she added that the new Connie had a face too ruddy, hair too dark, eyes too deep-sunk, and a chest too broad. Charley Ruminer, Tiller's father, added that while the new Connie's harmonica performances were much like those he remembered from the earlier Connie, they were lacking a certain element of style that the earlier Connie had possessed. Reporters also noted that the new Connie was mistaken about which cabin belonged to the Ruminer family, in spite of the fact that he had often visited their cabin when wooing Tiller months earlier.

Several of the doubters noted the difference in age between the Connie they remembered and the Connie they now saw. An old friend of Connie's, Coleman Foster, was brought in from Oklahoma to examine the man who said he was Connie Franklin. After examining him, Foster—who used to cut Connie's hair—said that the man was a fraud. He did not have a mole on the side of his neck which Foster distinctly remembered. In addition, his shoulders were too wide and his hair was too dark. Prosecutor Hugh Williamson noted that, even if Connie had not been murdered, clearly a crime of some sort had been committed, and it was his job to continue the prosecution until they had gotten to the bottom of the case. Accordingly, both prosecution and defense continued preparing for the murder trial that was scheduled to take place on December 16.

Meanwhile, how did the newly discovered Connie Franklin explain his disappearance? What he told questioners, and what he later would say in the courtroom, was that he had never been attacked by his good friends the defendants, but that together they had been celebrating the coming wedding and Connie had taken a bit too much drink. The bloody hat, and the bruises that had been noted on his body at the Wingo farm, were all a result of his having fallen off a mule after his excessive partying. It would seem that his fall caused him to change his mind about getting married, because he had voluntarily left the county, even leaving behind his few possessions, largely to escape the impending if not yet firmly scheduled wedding day. During the trial, he testified that he had visited Tiller the morning of March 10, that she had changed her mind and refused to marry him, and that her rejection of his proposal was the reason he suddenly left town.

Reporters who had missed the initial scoop of Connie's reappearance in Humphrey continued to research the man who had been found, and they were not slow to produce new revelations of interest. The man's name was not Connie Franklin, as he claimed; his real name was Marion Franklin Rogers. He was thirty-two years old, married, with three or four children. He had been drafted into the U.S. Army in 1926, but within a week of reporting for duty, he had been placed in the Arkansas State Hospital, diagnosed as mentally ill. In 1927, he had escaped from the hospital, and evidently he had been wandering the state of Arkansas ever since that escape.

Medical and dental records from the hospital, along with fingerprints and handwriting samples, established beyond doubt that the man who claimed to be Connie Franklin in December 1929 was indeed Marion Rogers. It was not so easy to prove or disprove that Marion Rogers had visited St. James for a few weeks at the beginning of that year claiming to be Connie Franklin. Tiller insisted that "her Connie" was not Marion Rogers, and some other residents agreed with her. Many other residents disagreed, including the defendants and their family and friends. As the day of the trial approached, and as reporters and other interested spectators gathered, the debate of "is he or isn't he Connie Franklin?" seemed unlikely to be easily resolved. Marion himself seemed to know his way around St. James as if he had lived there for a time, and he knew the personal details of the lives of some of his evident neighbors. If he had been given information so he could play the part of Connie Franklin, his instructors had prepared him well and he was a consummate actor.

A jury was selected on December 16, 1929, and the case of the murder of Connie Franklin was heard in Stone County Court on December 17 and 18, Judge S. Marcus Bone presiding. The days of the trial have been repeatedly described as having "a circus atmosphere." Several days of rain had turned the streets of Mountain View into a muddy mess. Now reporters and townspeople were greeted by purveyors of food and drink of various kinds, as well as merchants offering all manner of souvenirs, and even an outdoor evangelist or two. Those lucky enough to be seated in the courtroom heard the same evidence that had already been presented publicly, with a few interesting twists. Tiller Ruminer, spending two hours on the stand, repeated her sordid account of the nighttime assault of March 9. She admitted under questioning that she had not actually seen Connie thrown onto the fire or cut into pieces. She said that those details had been given to her by the defendants, perhaps boasting of their deeds but probably intending to frighten her in order to ensure her silence.

The testimony of Reuben Harrell was introduced. An interpreter from the Arkansas School for the Deaf in Little Rock, Mrs. R. L. Riggs, assisted with his testimony and with the examination from both attorneys. Through her, he described to the jury and to the crowd in the courtroom how he had seen Herman Greenway carrying the limp, possibly dead, body of Connie Franklin through the woods the night of March 9. The coffee can of bones taken from the pile of ashes was brought forth as evidence, but strangely the piece of bone that had been identified in Little Rock as part of a human skull was no longer in the container. A local dentist examined the remaining bones and testified that they probably came from a dog or a sheep.

On December 18, Marion Rogers took the stand and swore that he had lived for several weeks in St. James under the name of Connie Franklin and that he had courted Tiller Ruminer and planned to marry her under that name. He denied that he had been assaulted or beaten (let alone killed) by the defendants, and he repeated the account of having been injured on March 9 by falling off his mule after a time of drinking. Hester, Greenway, White, and Younger all agreed that they had not beaten or killed Connie but that they had poured a few drinks with him and that any damage that occurred to him had come from the fall off the back of his mule. They insisted that they had not seen Tiller or attacked her in any way that night. Several witnesses were called forward to vouch that Marion Rogers was the same man who had lived in St. James nearly a year before as Connie Franklin. The defense suggested that Harrell—who was known for "unimpeachable veracity"—had seen a drunken Connie carried by his friend but was not a witness to any murder. Ben Williamson further suggested that the four men were the victims of an eight-year feud and were not guilty of any of the crimes with which they were charged.

The jury, consisting of farmers from northern and western Stone County, considered what they had seen and heard for twenty hours before reaching a verdict. By December 19, the rain outdoors had turned to snow. At eleven o'clock that morning, they reported to Judge Bone that they were unable to reach a verdict, being deadlocked six to six, but the judge refused to accept their report. According to Judge Bone, $8,000 had been spent on this act of justice. Stone County was broke and could not afford to convene a second jury and try the case again. The jurors asked to hear their instructions again and also asked to hear again the testimony of Garrison regarding the bone fragments. Judge Bone answered one of the jury's concerns by promising that a separate trial would consider Tiller's charges of rape against Greenway and Hester. With that assurance, after meeting together and discussing further, the jury finally announced that they could not convict the four defendants of the charge of murder beyond a reasonable doubt.

The reporters filed their stories and went home. The merchants and preachers who had gathered on the courthouse square also returned to their homes. Charges were dropped against Alex Fulks, the alleged ringleader of the gang of murderers. The promised trial on the charges of rape was never held. For most people, life went on as it had before, and the questions about Connie Franklin became local lore and a matter of Arkansas trivia.

Three of the four defendants left the area. Herman Greenway and Hubert Hester settled on a farm in Mayes County, Oklahoma, in

1930. Joe White also lived for a few years in Oklahoma, and then moved farther west to California. Bill Younger stayed on the family farm in Stone County.

Tiller Ruminer also stayed in Stone County. She was already outside of her father's household at the time of the 1930 census. Records indicate that she married and had a family, and that they endured the same desperate poverty that Tiller had known with her parents and younger siblings.

If television had existed in 1929, Marion Rogers would have been on all the national talk shows after the trial ended. Instead, he pursued the Depression version of the same circuit. He appeared and spoke in public in Little Rock and other Arkansas cities, then branching out to be seen and heard in Oklahoma, Texas, and even Chicago. When his fame had expired, he returned to the same wandering life that he had known before his dramatic appearance. In December 1932, he was found lying by the side of a road outside of Clarendon, Arkansas. Taken to a boarding house in the city, he died there a few days later.

Information about the trial for the murder of Connie Franklin is drawn largely from newspaper accounts of the times. Local lore states that Judge Bone ordered the destruction of all court records not legally required to be saved immediately after the end of the trial, in order to bring an end to the gossip. Whether this assertion is true or not (and it seems unlikely that a judge would expect to end gossip by eradicating written evidence of what was said), the official court records of what happened during the trial are missing and therefore are not available to researchers.

Clearly some witnesses in the courtroom those December days were lying. Either Connie Franklin was attacked and brutally killed on March 9, 1929, or else he was not. Either Marion Rogers was the drifter who called himself Connie Franklin, the man who wooed and won Tiller's heart, or he was not. For the national reporters who covered the trial, the strange case lifted a veil which hid corruption in the heart of local Arkansas, revealing feudal baronage, peonage, and even worse abuses of the many by the few. For Arkansas's leaders, including Governor Parnell, and the local newspapers who followed his lead, these claims of baronage, peonage, and the like showed nothing more than outsiders' prejudices about Arkansas and were far from true or believable. If the governor was correct, then Bertha Burns and Tiller Ruminer created a sensational story for private reasons that may never be known. If the governor was wrong, then perhaps a few powerful families were able to pervert justice with the help of a surprisingly talented actor.

As is often the case with historical mysteries, the facts can be combined in a variety of ways to support a variety of explanations. Elmer Wingo's description of Connie's appearance at the Wingo farm shortly after the alleged murder seems to be at odds both with Tiller's accusations and with Marion Rogers's statements at the trial. In the end, when evidence is spotty and contradictory, a researcher's conclusions—about Connie Franklin, or about any other historical figure—may reveal more about the researcher than about what really happened.

Afterword and Bibliography

As mentioned in the foreword, each of the nine people described in this book is the subject of an entry in the Encyclopedia of Arkansas History & Culture—online at www.encyclopediaofarkansas.net. All nine of those entries are linked to additional entries about related people, places, events, and ideas. In addition, readers of this book who would like additional information about any of these people may find the following sources helpful. This afterword is not meant as a complete bibliography; it is meant more as a list of suggestions for anyone who is seeking additional information.

Some papers related to **Sandy Faulkner** are located in the Faulkner Family Collection, part of the J. N. Heiskell Collection in the University of Arkansas at Little Rock Archives in the Arkansas Studies Institute building in Little Rock. The standard biography of Faulkner was written by Margaret Smith Ross. Versions of it appeared in the *Arkansas Gazette* and the *Pulaski County Historical Review*, but probably the most easily available version of that biography is "Sanford C. Faulkner," in the *Arkansas Historical Review* 14 (Winter 1955), pages 301–315.

No single biography of **Charlie McDermott** has yet been written, but several books have collected articles about his life, including some of his own writings. The best sources of information about him are Rebecca DeArmond's *Old Times Not Forgotten: A History of Drew County* (Little Rock: Rose Publishing Company, 1980) and *Bartholomew's Song: A Bayou History* (Bowie, MD: Heritage Books, 2001), and Sheila Farrell Brannon's *Tribute to Chicot County, Arkansas* (Dermott: 2000).

Solon Borland is frequently mentioned in Margaret Smith Ross's book *Arkansas Gazette: The Early Years, 1819–1866* (Little Rock: Arkansas Gazette Foundation, 1969). He also receives significant attention in Michael Dougan's *Confederate Arkansas: The People and Policies of a Frontier State in Wartime* (Tuscaloosa: University of Alabama Press, 1976). The significance of his diplomatic career is addressed in William O. Scroggs's *Filibusters and Financiers: The Story of William Walker and His Associates* (New York: Macmillan Company, 1916).

Newspaperman **J. N. Smithee** is covered extensively in Michael Dougan's *Community Diaries: Arkansas Newspapering, 1819–2002* (Little Rock: August House, 2003) as well as Frederick Allsopp's *History of the Arkansas Press for a Hundred Years and More* (Little Rock: Parke-Harper Publishing Company, 1922). Of course significant information about Smithee appears in the various newspapers with which he was associated, especially the *Arkansas Gazette* and the *Arkansas Democrat*.

Information about **Sid Wallace** can be found in Lillian Mickel's four-volume work *History of Johnson County, Arkansas* (Clarksville, AR: 1983, 1984). His story is also told in Jim Phillips's article, "The Legend of Bloody Clarksville," *Johnson County Historical Review* 7 (October 1981), pages 1–8. Much of the legend is presented and interpreted in C. H. McKennon's *Iron Men: A Saga of the Deputy United States Marshals Who Rode the Indian Territory* (Garden City, NY: Doubleday & Company, 1967). Additional information can be found about Sid Wallace in newspaper articles from 1871 through 1874, especially from the days leading up to his execution.

Anyone interested in learning more about **Scipio Africanus Jones** can start with the file about Jones in the Tom W. Dillard Black Arkansiana Materials at the Butler Center for Arkansas Studies in the Arkansas Studies Institute building in Little Rock. Dillard's research about Jones also was published as "Scipio A. Jones" in the *Arkansas Historical Quarterly* 31 (Autumn 1972), pages 201–219. Jones also is mentioned prominently in Grif Stockley's *Blood in Their Eyes: The Elaine Race Massacres of 1919* (Fayetteville: University of Arkansas Press, 2001).

Bernie Babcock is the subject of Marcia Camp's "The Soul of Bernie Babcock" in the *Pulaski County Historical Review* 36 (Fall 1988), pages 50–62. Marcia Camp is currently writing a biography with the same title that will greatly enhance the public's memory of Bernie Babcock. The Bernie Babcock Remembrances are in the Special Collections at the University of Arkansas Libraries in Fayetteville. More information about Babcock's unique acquisitions for her museum has been published by Lloyd McCracken and Dan and Phyllis Morse as a four-part article titled, "Dentler Rowland and King Crowley and Those Mysterious Stone Images" in the *Craighead County Historical Quarterly* 42 and 43, from July 2004 through April 2005.

The papers of **John Brown Watson** are stored as the John Brown Papers in the John Hay Library Special Collections at Brown University in Providence, Rhode Island. Additional information about Doc Watson can be found on the campus of the University of Arkansas at Pine Bluff. Much information about his career, especially his years at AM&N, is printed in Frederick Chambers's "Historical Study of Arkansas Agricultural, Mechanical, and Normal College, 1873–1943," a doctoral thesis written at Ball State University in 1970.

Finally, the odd story of **Connie Franklin** is drawn largely from the newspapers of 1929. The best summary of the story is Brooks Blevins's "The Arkansas Ghost Trial: The Connie Franklin Case and the Ozarks in the National Media," in the *Arkansas Historical Quarterly* 68 (Autumn 2009), pages 245–271. Blevins also addresses the matter of Connie Franklin in his book *Arkansas/Arkansaw: How Bear Hunters, Hillbillies, and Good Ol' Boys Defined a State* (Fayetteville: University of Arkansas Press, 2009).

Index

About the Author

Steven Teske is an archival assistant at the Butler Center for Arkansas Studies, part of the Central Arkansas Library System. He was formerly the fact-checker for the Butler Center's *Encyclopedia of Arkansas History & Culture*. He is also an adjunct instructor for the Arkansas State University–Beebe campus located at the Little Rock Air Force Base and has taught classes for Pulaski Technical College. He is co-author, with Velma B. Branscum Woody, of *Homefront Arkansas: Arkansans Face Wartime*. Currently, he is writing a collection of Arkansas biographies for elementary school students. Mr. Teske lives with his wife and seven children in North Little Rock.

CPSIA information can be obtained
at www.ICGtesting.com
Printed in the USA
FSHW021854250519

9 781935 106357